A pineapple a day keeps the worries away

On first inspection, the midday heat of a scorching tropical day doesn't seem like the ideal grounds for crafting. However, to me, tropical means projects that pop with colour and are specific to a very special season: High Summer. The hazy heat of summer brings the need to replenish often by escaping the sun with a glass of something cool enough that there's condensation on the glass. A day of basking in the midday sun with regular retreats to the shade for a few more rounds of crochet is just the replenishment this crafter needs.

Our summer handmade wardrobes deserve as much attention as that which we bestow on our garments the rest of the year. Tropical projects that come to mind are whimsical and defined by the intensity of the heat: beach cover-ups, a wrap for the cooler yet still balmy evenings and perhaps a pair of espadrilles? We've got all of these ideas covered in this issue as well as plenty of small projects that won't feel too hot to handle as temperatures rise. For my challenge, I'm taking inspiration from nature's most beautiful tones with a hummingbird pocket for a small tablet device. It's time to celebrate nature's richest tones and let the light in.

COMMISSIONED BY

Scheepjes

scheepjes.com

CONCEPT, STYLING & ART DIRECTION
Marita Janssen
GRAPHIC DESIGN
Suzanne Nuis
CREATIVE DIRECTORS SCHEEPJES
Anita Mundt & Simy Somer
TEXT, TRANSLATION AND EDITING
Christa Veenstra, Flory Hartog
PHOTOGRAPHY
Violaine Chappallaz
Dana van Leeuwen
Ernst Yperlaan
MAKE-UP ARTIST
Peter Dekker, Hanneke de Hertog
MODELS
Mary/Eefjevandaal Luca/Kiki/SpecialMax
DESIGNERS
Bernadette Ambergen, Esther de Beer, Rachele Carmona, Carmen Jorissen, Sarah Knight, Tatsiana Kupryianchyk, Maria McPherson, Nerissa Muijs, Atty van Norel, Dedri Uys, Christa Veenstra, Jellina Verhoeff.

FOR INQUIRIES ABOUT YARN
simy@simysstudio.com
Mercuriusweg 16
NL 9482 WL Tynaarlo
The Netherlands

Language: Dutch and English
Publication: twice a year
ISBN 9789491840128

This little icon indicates the relevant page number for the instructions for each design. The workbook starts on page 49.

CONTENTS

04 PLANT HOUSE
04 SUMMER COVER-UP
06 CACTUS PUZZLE BALLS
08 GREENHOUSE TOP
10 AMAZON BLANKET

16 EXOTIC FRUITS
17 STAR FRUIT BLANKET
18 PINEAPPLE GARLAND
20 TROPICAL FLOWER POUF
22 WALL-HANGING FRUIT

27 BIRDS OF PARADISE
28 BIRDS OF PARADISE SHAWL
31 CLUB TROPICANA BAG
32 HUMMINGBIRD CARDIGAN

38 COCKTAIL HOUR
39 MANHATTAN CLUTCH
40 PIÑA COLADA SHAWL
42 MOJITO ESPADRILLES
44 TEQUILA SUNRISE TOWELS

49 WORKBOOK
76 NOTES
80 SCRAPBOOK

IN THIS ISSUE
12 MAKING THE CUT - About scissors
24 INSPIRING ARTISTS - Kaffe Fasset & Studio Roof
34 BLOGGER'S FAVOURITES - Christa Veenstra
36 A SINGLE MOTIF - Christa Veenstra
37 SIMY'S CHALLENGE - Crafting evolution
46 BOOKS - Ribbon embroidery

Plant
HOUSE

Summer Cover-up

BY SARAH KNIGHT

The perfect summer companion. Made from soft cotton, this shawl is lightweight and breathable. Colour and texture blocks add an element of interest and fun to any outfit. Compact to carry on a day trip out to cover your shoulders from the blazing sun or your modesty on the beach.

YARN: SCHEEPJES COTTON 8

50

CACTUS PUZZLE BALLS

BY DEDRI UYS

Mini terracotta pots 6.5cm €0.65 - *dille-kamille.nl*

54

It's always the small pieces that make the big picture

Tiny Amish puzzle balls create decorative and playful everlasting plants that brighten any interior. The accompanying video puts the final puzzle piece to the pattern.

YARN: SCHEEPJES MAXI BONBON

Light blue jeans - pepejeans.com

Greenhouse Top

BY CARMEN JORISSEN

Inspired by greenhouse foliage, the Greenhouse top is made almost entirely from plant-based fibres. Like the ridges on a leaf, the pattern creates symmetrical lines that wrap around the body.

YARN: SCHEEPJES LINEN SOFT

51

As the heat rises, crochet your own Amazon journey using interlocking motifs in five brightly coloured panels to create an explosion of colour.

YARN: SCHEEPJES SOFTFUN AND SOFTFUN DENIM

56

Dress with green stripes - oililyworld.com

Amazon Blanket

BY RACHELE CARMONA

Making THE CUT

BY ESTHER DE BEER

FOUND IN NEARLY EVERY KITCHEN DRAWER IN THE WORLD AND INDISPENSABLE TO ANY SEAMSTRESS, KNITTER, CROCHETER AND EMBROIDERER: A GOOD PAIR OF SCISSORS. AT FIRST GLANCE, SCISSORS ARE ONLY CUT OUT TO, WELL, CUT. BUT THE POINT IS: EVERY TYPE OF CRAFT REQUIRES A SPECIFIC TYPE OF SCISSORS TO GUARANTEE THE BEST RESULT.

Various Internet sources honour the illustrious artist Leonardo da Vinci as the inventor of scissors. But this turns out to be nothing more than a persistent myth, for scissors have been around long before Da Vinci was even born. The first type of shears were found in the hands of the Egyptians. These consisted of just two blades, connected by a narrow strip of bronze that also formed the handle. Not exactly ergonomic, but it got the job done. Through the following centuries, iron processing evolved and so did scissors: the blades were bent and sharpened, resulting in scissors with sharp-edged blades that perfectly aligned and that were well cut out for precision work. However, it wasn't until after the industrial revolution that scissors found a home in the kitchen drawer of almost every household, from rich to poor.

SCISSORS ARE SCISSORS, OR ARE THEY?

Having one pair of scissors for every type of craft is like only having one pan for cooking. It just won't do the job. Every crafter will agree: for every type of craft, there is a specific type of scissors that guarantees the best results. It is a well-known fact that seamstresses will frantically guard their fabric scissors from ignorant hands trying to use these on materials like plastic or paper, and rightfully so. Most fabric scissors are equipped with at least one serrated blade, which has a firm grip on fabric and doesn't slide on the worktop. Cutting other materials than fabric will definitely blunt the blades, basically ruining the entire tool. All fabric shears have one flat side, keeping the scissors steady and making it easy to cut along pattern pieces and in straight lines. Analysing the anatomy of scissors, the pivot point proves to be the Achilles heel of many shears, as under high pressure or force the pivot loosens causing the blades to wobble and fabric to mangle or warp. Fabric shears with blades connected by a patented Allen key have proven to be far more stable, leading to smoothly cutting through all types of fabric. Pinking shears are reliable partners for finishing fabric edges, preventing them to fray. Cutting fabric on the bias will keep it from fraying, so for quilters or seamstresses that don't like sewing a zigzag, pinking scissors are friends for life.

SNIP SNAP

A small pair of scissors is a must-have in any project bag, a pair with razor sharp little blades and a very pointy tip. They are just the best for cutting small threads or opening buttonholes. Embroidery scissors are a perfect match for these types of tasks, as the blades are short, sharp and pointed, making them extremely manoeuvrable. They make perfect little 'snips' in fabric, or any material for that matter. Embroiderers love their small scissors as they snip off embroidery threads short and neatly, and for that same reason, these types of scissors are found in plenty of crochet and knitting bags: after all, yarn that is sharply cut is so much easier to weave in than fraying ends.

LOVING THE LEFTIES

Those who are left handed know all too well: looking for a left-handed pair of scissors that actually works and is comfortable as well, is like looking for that famous needle in the equally famous haystack. Some left-handed people loathe left-handed scissors so much, they end up teaching themselves how to use 'normal' shears in their right hand instead: less of a fuss and more scissors to choose from. The problem with many pairs of scissors for left-handed people is that manufacturers simply switch the handle on normal scissors from right to left handed, but this is not enough. A good left-handed pair of scissors also has the blades placed the other way around: the right blade shouldn't be on top, but the left blade should. This in combination with the left-handed handle makes for a great pair of shears for lefties. →

1
2
premax
3
4
RING-LOCK
Made in Italy
premax
5
9

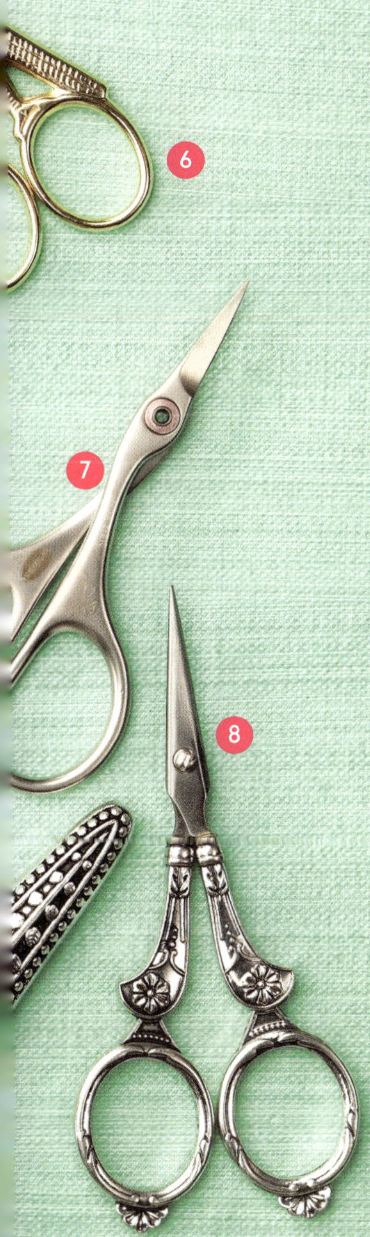

1. PREMAX OPTIMA 8

ART. 6772-834

The perfect pair of fabric shears for left handed people, including left-handed blades and left-handed handles, and not expensive either.

2. PREMAX RING-LOCK PROFESSIONAL

ART. 6917-1000

The 'Rolls Royce' among scissors. These are available in many sizes, from large to embroidery size. The blades will never start wobbling, due to the clever Allan key pivot point. The open spaces in the blades will conduct warmth during cutting. The grip is very comfortable.

3. MUNDIAL CUSHION SOFT

ART. 311250-01

An ideal pair of scissors for seamstresses and dressmakers. With the help of the serrated blades the Mundial easily cut through literally dozens of layers of fabric, without moving or mangling it. The Mundial are sold including a small pair of scissors.

4. PREMAX DRESSMAKING SHEARS

ART. F11970800

Dressmaking shears like we saw our mother and grandmothers use them. Still going strong, especially in this modern version: very refined serrated blades, extremely steady and trustworthy when cutting long ends of fabric.

5. PREMAX RING-LOCK PINKING SHEARS

ART. 6362-800

Most pinking shears are heavy and rigid. But not these ones. The Ring-Lock pinking shears are flexible and far lighter than other pinking shears. They also have the clever Allen key pivot point.

6. PREMAX EMBROIDERY SCISSORS

ART. 7125-312

So nice to look at and so wonderful to use. Perfect to cut open buttonholes and get rid of small threads. Extremely manoeuvrable.

7. SHEARS

ART. 1910-334

This little pair of scissors will last for decades, maybe even generations. Small, sharp and manoeuvrable, including all the clever pros of the larger Ring-Lock scissors.

8. DELUXE EMBROIDERY SCISSORS

ART. 97257

If you love vintage and retro, you basically need a pair of scissors like this in your craft box. The design is pure nostalgia and the quality is top notch. The blades and tip are razor sharp. When cutting threads, you will hear this wonderful snipping sound. Also perfect for crocheters and knitters.

9. SIMY'S STUDIO EMBROIDERY SCISSORS WITH CHAIN

ART. 96672

You will never be looking for your pair of embroidery scissors again, there come in a spectacularly beautiful case with chain. It's retro, almost Art Nouveau. The blades and tip are nice and sharp.

Exotic FRUITS

STAR FRUIT BLANKET

BY ATTY VAN NOREL

This fruity throw in watermelon colours is created from a natural cotton fibre with a soft sun-bleached effect. The join-as-you-go segments can be repeated to create any size of blanket you choose.

YARN: SCHEEPJES CATONA DENIM

59

Bowl of woven plastic thread - *kitschkitchen.nl*

Pineapple GARLAND

BY NERISSA MUIJS

64

Create a new family tradition by inviting this tropical garland to all your summer parties. From birthdays to barbeques, add a little zing!

YARN: SCHEEPJES SOFTFUN AND SOFTFUN DENIM

Pineapple fold-out - *kitschkitchen.nl*

Based on a textured mandala design, this colourful pouf adds a pop of colour to any interior. Instant joy!

MATERIAAL: SCHEEPJES BLOOM

60

Tropical FLOWER POUF

BY TATSIANA KUPRYIANCHYK

Yellow fruit bowl - klevering.nl

WALL-HANGING *Fruit*

BY JELLINA VERHOEFF

Green Pineapple lamp and porcelain dish (p.23) - *klevering.nl*

An optical illusion creates a masterpiece of your crochet. Inspired by pineapple skin, these tessellating shapes fit together to produce a bold statement on your wall.

YARN: SCHEEPJES CATONA

62

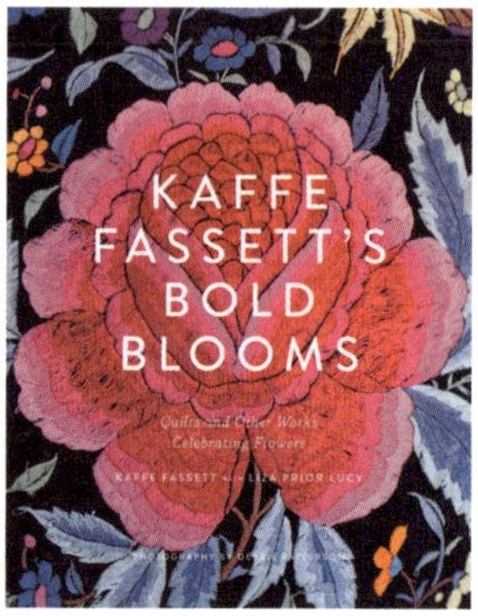

Kaffe Fassett's Bold Blooms, by Kaffe Fassett and Liza Prior Lucy (Abrams, £21.99)

KAFFE FASSET

- DESIGNER -

"I cannot express in words what colour means to me"

Textile artist Kaffe Fassett (79) lives for his art. After fifty years of working continuously, his oeuvre is large and impressive, as is his reputation as a passionate lover of colour.

Kaffe was already in his thirties when he cast on his first garment. He was sold on it immediately. From that first sweater, textile and thread in all their variations were the materials he has worked with until this very day. 'From very early on, I had been painting but when I had knitted that first sweater, I was hooked. The fact that in knitting you could play with colours so beautifully brought me to the art of needlepoint and from there to patchwork and quilting, designing my own printed fabrics.'

His colourful designs, ranging from garments to quilts to man-size needlepoint tapestries, made him a celebrated artist. His work has been exhibited in many leading museums all over the world. Apart from creating his own works, he has also received commissions from well-known fashion houses, celebrities like Lauren Bacall, Barbra Streisand and Shirley Maclaine, and from miscellaneous companies and organizations. And whether he is designing costumes for a ballet company or a garden for the Chelsea Flower Show, colour will always be his trademark. 'I cannot explain what colour means to me. Colour enriches my life; there's no other way of explaining the magic of colour.

This doesn't mean I could never make anything in black and white. The lack of colour in white and black containing all colours makes for an exciting combination.' Kaffe may be almost 80, but his dreams are as big as ever: 'Covering a skyscraper in mosaics would be amazing or making a huge tapestry.....as long as it is something magnificent!' Is it all about recognition, the enormous proportions of such a work? The answer is as surprising as it is modest: 'I'm happiest when working; when I'm not working on a project, I feel lost. The biggest compliment I can get is when people are touched by my work and find inspiration to create something themselves.'
kaffefassett.com

STUDIO ROOF

- DESIGNERS -

"Our designs are honest and authentic"

What constitutes the world of Studio Roof? The answer is: buildings, cars, people, rockets, but mostly cartboard animals and plants. All as colourful as they are poetic and suitable for all ages.

'A completely white interior? No, that doesn't make me happy', Romy Boesveldt (48) smiles. 'This doesn't mean that at home all the walls have different colours, but there's a lot of art and there are small interesting objects brought home from our travels everywhere. Studio Roof's own creations have their place too of course: I love our own work.' Studio Roof's story begins in 2005 when Romy and her husband Ilya Yashkin (49), originally an architect, designed and started selling a cartboard playhouse that you can paint yourself. It was a great success. Twelve years on and Romy and Ilya's products can be found in shops all over the world. Romy: 'Our signature style is the use of colour and working three dimensionally. That's mainly Ilya's brainpower. Apart from being colourful and playful, our designs are also basic, honest and natural.' Asking how they decide on the colours for their designs, Romy falls silent for a moment. 'It's not science; the colour combinations develop intuitively and through trial and error. It's always a search: together we sit in front of the computer screen and experiment with all kinds of colours until something we're happy with emerges.' At first glance you might think that all those imaginative creations are solely for children. 'Thankfully not! There are many adults that appreciate and buy our products.' The world-famous and ultrachic fashion brand Hermès is a fan too. Each year Studio Roof is commissioned to make a number of unique designs for Petit h, a part of Hermès that puts together an exclusive annual sales exhibition with designs made from Hermès' rest material. 'That's a great honour of course! It's proof that people recognize that we are authentic and create honest work. That feels like an enormous compliment.'

studioroof.com

BIRDS OF *Paradise*

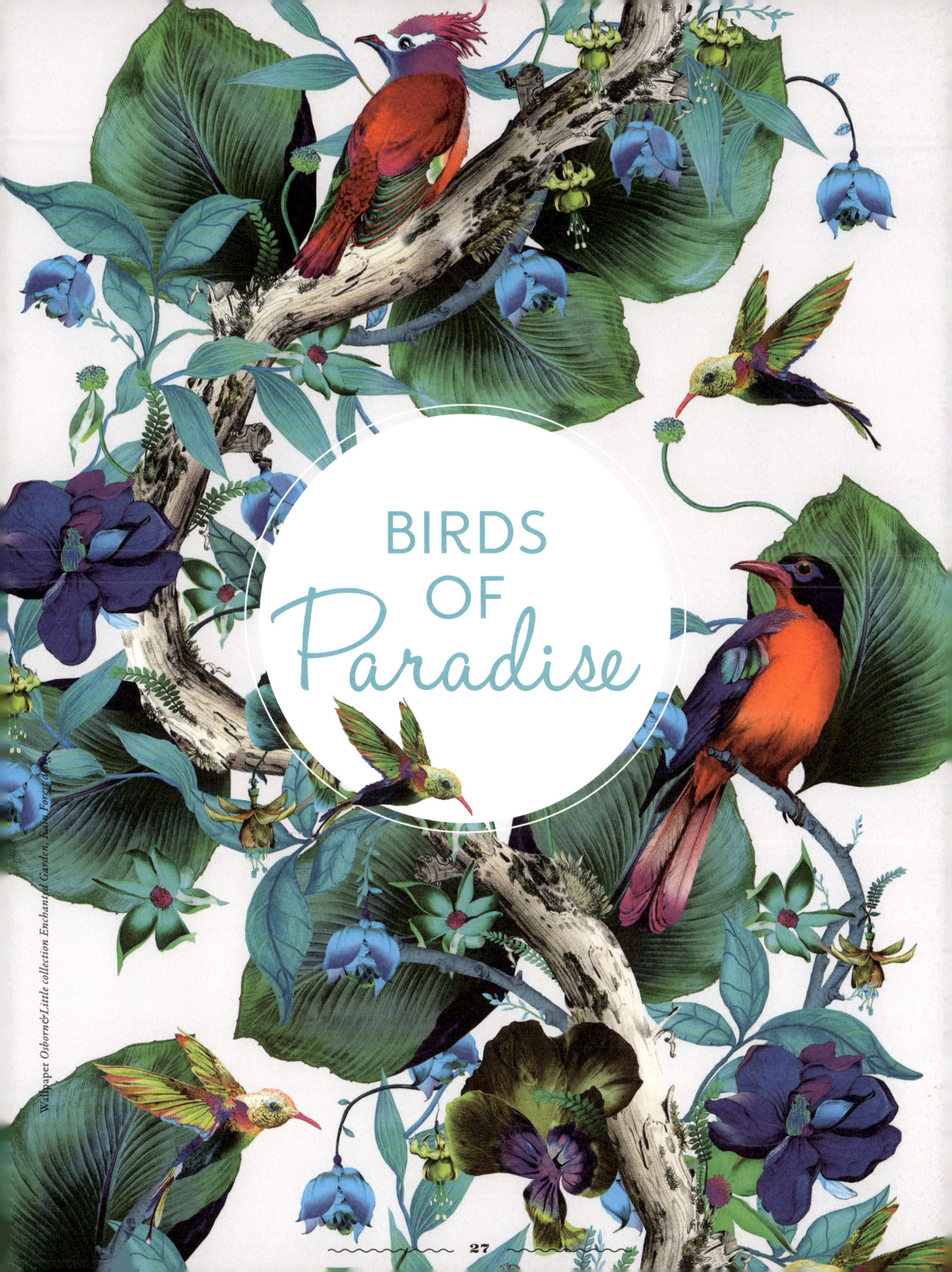

Wallpaper *Osborne&Little* collection *Enchanted Garden, Rain Forest design*

Birds of Paradise Shawl

BY BERNADETTE AMBERGEN

A dovetailed feature adds an unexpected detail to one side of this shawl. Select a riot of colours and let them sing!

YARN: SCHEEPJES COTTON 8

65

Chair, *meubelstofferderij-sarab.nl*, beach dress *pepejeans.com*

SPREAD YOUR WINGS AND LEARN TO FLY
Woven cotton skirt and top *oililyworld.com*

Wallpaper Osborne&Little collection Enchanted Garden, [illegible] design -info@vva.nl

With plenty of space for all your summer accessories, this striking bag is as light as a feather. Finish with a coconut shell button, pull the strings and off you go.

FABRIC: TISSU DE MARIE

66

Club Tropicana Bag

BY ESTHER DE BEER

Hummingbird Cardigan

BY CARMEN JORISSEN

Garment virgins will flock to crochet this cardigan, taking a basic motif construction and making it into something wearable. Team up with a bikini or a pair of jeans.

YARN: SCHEEPJES SUNKISSED

68

Bikini *pepejeans.com*

BLOGGER'S **FAVOURITES**

CHRISTA VEENSTRA

THECURIOCRAFTSROOM.BLOGSPOT.COM

On Christa's blog you'll find an overview of all her crochet designs and it is where she publishes free patterns. "I never imagined that crochet would become such a large part of my life and that I can share it with a wonderful international crafting community that is open to everyone's creativity."

YARN

Scheepjes Catona is the yarn I love best. It has a wonderful sheen and there are no less than 105 shades to choose from, so I can always find the right colour combinations.

INSPIRATION

When I started designing a few years ago, I thought it would be nice to work around a very specific theme and colour palette that would allow me to create different kinds of designs. The shape and colours of peacock feathers have always fascinated me so I now use them as my main source of inspiration.

THE HORTUS IN LEIDEN

The Hortus botanicus Leiden takes you back in time. Right in the heart of the city centre, you can enjoy the most beautiful tropical plants. Built in 1590 and lovingly maintained, it's an oasis of peace. With a restaurant and shop, it's my best tip for a day filled with inspiration.

www.hortusleiden.nl/en

KING OF FASHION

It' has become somewhat of a trend for famous fashion designers to use crochet and knitting in their garments. I really love this design by Alexander McQueen and would like to wear it myself.

ART NOUVEAU

I love the natural forms, curved lines and colours in Art Nouveau. These tiles were the inspiration for my latest peacock feather design.

TIP

Colouring books are a great way to experiment with new colour combinations.

CROCHET PORTRAITS

I wish I could 'paint' with yarn the way Jo Hamilton does. Her larger than life portraits are awe-inspiring and created directly from photographs without any charts or patterns. On her Facebook page she provides inspiring insights into her work.

'I TRADED PAINT AND A BRUSH FOR YARN AND A HOOK'

JO HAMILTON

PEACOCK MOTIF

BY CHRISTA VEENSTRA

MATERIALS
Scheepjes Linen Soft (47% cotton, 27% linen, 26% acrylic, 50g/135m)
1 ball each of:
Yarn A: 602
Yarn B: 611
Yarn C: 605
Yarn D: 606
Yarn E: 627
3.5mm crochet hook

MEASUREMENTS
14cm x 14cm (6.5in x 6.5in)

PATTERN NOTES
After the first few rounds, the motif will probably be all curled up. This will be partly rectified in the next few rounds and blocking will make the square entirely flat.

INSTRUCTIONS
With Yarn A make a magic ring wide enough to hold 24 dc and leave a long tail at the end not coming from the ball.

Round 1 24dc in ring, ss in first dc.

Round 2 Join Yarn B with 1dc in any dc, *(ch2, 1dc in next dc) 5 times, ch3, 1dc in next dc; rep from * 3 more times but miss final dc on last rep, ss in first dc.

Round 3 Join Yarn C with *(1dc, ch3, 1dc = corner) in any ch-3 sp, ch1, (1dc in next ch-2 sp, ch3) 4 times, 1dc in next ch-2 sp, ch1; rep from * 3 more times, ss in first dc.

Round 4 Join Yarn D in any corner ch-3 sp and work *(1tr, ch5, 1tr), ch3, (1dc in next ch-3 sp, ch3) 4 times; rep from * 3 more times, ss in first tr.

Round 5 Join Yarn B with *1dc in tr made before a ch5, (1htr, 7tr, 1htr) in ch-5 sp, 1dc in tr, ch2, (1dc in next dc, ch3) 3 times, 1dc in next dc, ch2; rep from * 3 more times, ss in first dc.

Round 6 Join Yarn D with *1dc in tr made before a ch5 in Round 4 and in which a dc was worked in Round 5 (this means the dc sits next to or partly covers the dc of Round 5), miss dc worked in tr in Round 5, 1dc in htr and in each of the next 3 tr, (1dc, ch3, 1dc) in next tr, 1dc in each of the next 3 tr and in next htr, miss dc worked in tr in Round 5, 1dc in tr, 2dc around ch-3 sp of Round 4 and ch-2 sp of Round 5, ch2, (1dc around ch-3 sp of Round 4 and ch-3 sp of Round 5, ch2) 3 times, 2dc around ch-3 sp of Round 4 and ch-2 sp of Round 5; rep from * 3 more times, ss in first dc.

Round 7 Join Yarn E with *(1dc, ch2, 1dc) in any corner ch-3 sp, 6dc blo, ch3, miss (2 dc, ch-2 sp, 1 dc), 1dc in next ch-2 sp, ch3, 1dc in next ch-2 sp, ch3, miss (1 dc, ch-2 sp, 2 dc), 6dc blo; rep from * 3 more times, ss in first dc.

Round 8 Join Yarn A with *(1dc, ch2, 1dc) in any corner ch-2 sp, 6dc blo ch5, miss (1 dc, ch-3 sp, 1 dc), 1dc in next ch-3 sp, ch5, miss (1 dc, ch-3 sp, 1 dc), 6dc blo; rep from * 3 more times, ss in first dc.

Round 9 Continue with Yarn A, ss in corner ch-2 sp, ch1, *(1dc, ch2, 1dc) in same corner ch-2 sp, 6dc in ch-5 sp, 1dc, 6dc in ch-5 sp, 7dc; rep from * 3 more times, ss in first dc.

TO FINISH
Weave in all ends, block the motif and allow to dry naturally.

Simy's
CHALLENGE

CRAFTING EVOLUTION

Breathing new life into a long-forgotten craft (or at least long forgotten by me) is always an exciting turn of events. Using traditional techniques in new ways or with modern materials marries together generations of crafters and brings their work into today's spotlight.

I remember many years ago when at art college, pouring over detailed images of French and Belgian embroidery. Seeing how small pieces of fabric, lace and ribbon brought dimension to the stitches captured my attention.

Recently I was gifted this beautiful handmade tablet case by Yorkshire crafter Liz Barraclough. Using a small piece of hand-painted silk fabric as a backdrop for her embroidery, she completed the beautiful image by adding dimension with ribbon embroidery. It instantly took my mind back to those old images I had seen while studying.

Every crafter I know, whether a paper crafter, yarn crafter or fabric crafter has copious amounts of ribbon in their stash: ribbons they have bought, ribbons they've kept that have adorned gifts, ribbons that may have previously had another purpose. We all have precious ribbons that look beautiful but we don't always know what to do with them.

The age-old technique of ribbon embroidery is a perfect way to use your ribbon stash. By simply sewing a length of ribbon into an embroidery, looping strands of ribbon over to create depth and texture or even trying your hand at some simple flowers stitched with the ribbon itself, you are borrowing techniques from the past. The wide variety of ribbons available in bright and vibrant colours brings this 'old' technique onto today's crafting table.

My challenge for you is to dig out your stashed ribbons and find new and creative ways to use it. You might even try your hand at a little ribbon embroidery. Take a photo of your makes and #SimysChallenge on Instagram so I, and others, can see and be inspired by your creative ribbon use.

INSTAGRAM #SIMYSCHALLENGE
www.simysstudio.com

Cocktail HOUR

MANHATTAN CLUTCH

BY SARAH KNIGHT

Put on your high heels, paint your nails and pick up this luxurious, knitted bag for an exciting evening on the town.

YARN: SCHEEPJES SECRET GARDEN

70

Skirt, shoes and sweater primark.com

PIÑA COLADA SHAWL

BY NERISSA MUIJS

Learn how to crochet short rows whilst making this crescent shawl. The unique colours in this silk blended yarn make every shawl one of a kind.

YARN: SCHEEPJES SECRET GARDEN

72

Shirt with feathers pepejeans.com, skirt with palm print oililyworld.com

MOJITO ESPADRILLES

BY NERISSA MUIJS

Keep your cool as the temperature rises in a pair of hand-crocheted espadrilles. Purchase soles to suit your size and choose from our 87 Bonbon and Sugar Rush shades to match your shoes to your outfit.

YARN: SCHEEPJES MAXI SUGAR RUSH AND MAXI BONBON

74

Save water
Drink cocktails

TEQUILA SUNRISE TOWELS

BY MARIA MCPHERSON

Biocotton towel 70x140 cm €14,95 - *dille-kamille.nl*

Customize a beach towel with
your own 'dip-dyed' effect.
Will you go sunrise or sunset?

YARN: SCHEEPJES MAXI BONBON

76

These books will help you on your way:

RIBBON EMBROIDERY TRANSFERS
Marsha Michler
With 178 Iron-On Transfers
56 pages
ISBN 9780486298184

BEGINNER'S GUIDE TO SILK RIBBON EMBROIDERY
Ann Cox
A step-by-step approach with many photographs suited to first-time embroiderers
48 pages
ISBN 9781782211600

RIBBON EMBROIDERY & STUMPWORK
Di van Niekerk
30 flower models with clear illustrations by this professional South African textile artist
128 pages
ISBN 9781782213499

Free pattern downloads by artist Di van Niekerk can be found at www.dicraft.co.za.

RIBBON EMBROIDERY

In the Victorian era it was 'hot & happening', and now, over a hundred years later, ribbon embroidery is making its comeback. Rococo embroidery, as this technique is also called, is embroidery using ribbon. No other embroidery technique can create such lively, three-dimensional flowers and plants like this very special technique.

By varying ribbon widths, by interchanging ribbon with thread or by embroidering with the ribbon itself on the underlying fabric, it is as if you are painting with different sized brushes. An image transferred onto the fabric forms the basis. The possibilities are endless when it comes to the subject of your embroidery: you can draw an image yourself, or you can use a pre-designed image you iron onto the fabric. Standard images are usually flowers, plants and small figures. Let your imagination run wild and design your own image: a kitchen table scene with teapot, your child's favourite cartoon character, your pet, anything goes. Ribbon embroidery brings all kinds of scenes to life.

Ribbon embroidery works best using an embroidery hoop, preferably a ring in which you can stretch the fabric to achieve the correct tension. You start with the basic stitches: the ribbon stitch, the French knot and the straight stitch. With these stitches you can make wonderful flowers like geraniums and roses but also cornflowers. Regular embroidery threads can be used to make stems and add small decorations or any other details, thus creating special shapes and textures. There are many detailed stitches, all with beautiful names like fly stitch, Lazy Daisy stitch and fully open rose. Select your own set of favourite stitches or design some yourself!

If you master the basic techniques and enjoy embroidery work, you may have found a new interest for life. Ribbon embroidery can be easily combined with regular embroidery, but also with sewing, knitting, crocheting, quilting, or making 3D cards. These days, the most beautiful ribbons are available that previous generations did not have access to. Ribbons with prints, with differences in sheen and with gradients so that you can achieve completely different effects. The 3D-effect of the technique creates deep texture that really stands out and makes for an interesting result. As ribbon embroidery is a lesser known crafting technique, a gift made using this technique will surely become cherished.

Online, many ribbon embroidery pictures and examples can be found. The technique can be easily learned from books due to the many illustrations these contain so that even a beginner will be able to master it quickly.

Whirl

THIS DELICIOUS GRADIENT YARN FROM SCHEEPJES COMES IN 12 SCRUMPTIOUS COLOUR WAYS.

This delicious gradient yarn from Scheepjes comes in 12 scrumptious colour ways. Made from a blend of 60% cotton/40% acrylic to produce projects that are lightweight and breathable.
Unlike other gradient yarns, Whirl has a generous twist to enable speed while working the yarn and to help prevent splitting.

The beautiful drape of this yarn makes it perfect for shawls, accessories, garments and stylish home décor projects. This Extra Large yarn cake holds an enormous 1000 meters of softly colour changing yarn, more than enough for a large shawl or wrap.
Each colour change is carefully tied in an optimum way to ensure the knot can be discretely hidden within your stitches.

RECOMMENDED HOOK/NEEDLE SIZE 3.5-4.0MM

R.R.P. GBP 20.99 / USD 25.99

AVAILABLE VIA YOUR SCHEEPJES RETAILER

PATTERNS

FOR EACH PATTERN IN THE WORKBOOK THE SKILL LEVEL IS INDICATED WITH 1, 2 OR 3 SMALL PINEAPPLES.

1 pineapple means easy and
3 pineapples means it's a design
for the more advanced crafter.

Enjoy!

SUMMER COVER-UP

BY
Sarah Knight
craftsfromthecwtch.co.uk

MEASUREMENTS
Wingspan 195cm (78in)
Depth at point 90cm (36in)
(excluding fringe).

ABBREVIATIONS
See back cover flap

MATERIALS

Scheepjes Cotton 8 (100% cotton, 50g/170m)
1 ball each of:
Yarn A: 713
Yarn B: 665
Yarn C: 724
Yarn D: 723
Yarn E: 642
Yarn F: 517
Yarn G: 669
Yarn H: 715
Yarn I: 716
Yarn J: 650
4mm circular needle 100cm (40in) long
Stitch marker or safety pin
Tapestry needle
Crochet hook to apply fringe - suggested size 5mm

GAUGE/TENSION

18 sts and 26 rows to 10 x10cm in garter stitch using 4mm needles.

MEASUREMENTS

To alter the size, increase or decrease the number of pattern reps in each section, but note that this will affect the amount of yarn required.

SPECIAL ABBREVIATION

sl1 wyif move the working yarn to the front of the work (as if to purl) slip one stitch purlwise, then turn the work.

PATTERN NOTES

The cover-up is made from side to side using alternating garter stitch and lace sections, with each section made from a different colour. The colour order is indicated in the materials list. After the initial set-up, the last stitch on every row is slipped with the yarn held to the front of the work. There is an increase on every **RS** row. Place a marker or safety pin onto the **RS** of the work to help distinguish this reversible fabric.

INSTRUCTIONS

Set-up

With Yarn A, cast on 1 st.

Row 1 (RS) Kfb. [2 sts]
Row 2 (WS) K1, sl1wyif.
Row 3 K1, kfb. [3 sts]
Row 4 K to last st, sl1wyif.
Row 5 K1, kfb, sl1wyif. [4 sts]
Row 6 and every WS row As Row 4.
Row 7 K1, kfb, k1, sl1wyif. [5 sts]
Row 9 K1, kfb, k to last st, sl1wyif. [6 sts]
Row 11 As Row 9
Rep last 2 rows until there are 23 sts ending after a **WS** row.

Lace Section

NB: The colour change happens after the fourth st of the first lace row **ONLY**, on subsequent reps do not change colour.

Lace row 1 (WS) first time: K1, kfb, k1, change to next colour, k1, (yo, k2tog) to last st, sl1wyif.
Lace row 1 (WS) subsequent reps K1, kfb, k2, (yo, k2tog) to last st, sl1wyif.
Lace rows 2 and 4 K to last st, sl1wyif.
Lace row 3 K1, kfb, k2, (yo, k2tog) to last 2 sts, k1, sl1wyif.
Lace row 5 K1, kfb, k2, (yo, k2tog) to last st, sl1wyif.
Rep Lace rows 2 to 5 fifteen times (ending after row 5 to increase by 15 sts in this section).

Garter Section

Cut yarn leaving a tail for sewing in, then change to next colour in the materials list.
Garter row 1 (WS) K to last st, sl1wyif.
Garter row 2 K1, kfb, k to last st, sl1wyif.
Rep Garter rows 1 and 2 seventeen times (to increase by 17 sts in this section).
Rep Lace and Garter sections until all ten colours have been used, ending after a Lace section.

TO FINISH

Continuing with same colour yarn, knit as 'Garter Row 1' twice.
Cast off loosely (use a larger needle if necessary).

Fringe

Using remaining yarn, cut into pieces of 30cm (12in) lengths. Randomly mix the colours to make fringes with three strands each. Fold each of the fringes in half and, using a crochet hook, pull the central loop through the edge of the wrap. ♦

GREENHOUSE TOP

BY
Carmen Jorissen
craftyqueens.nl

MEASUREMENTS
See schematic

ABBREVIATIONS
See back cover flap

GREENHOUSE TOP

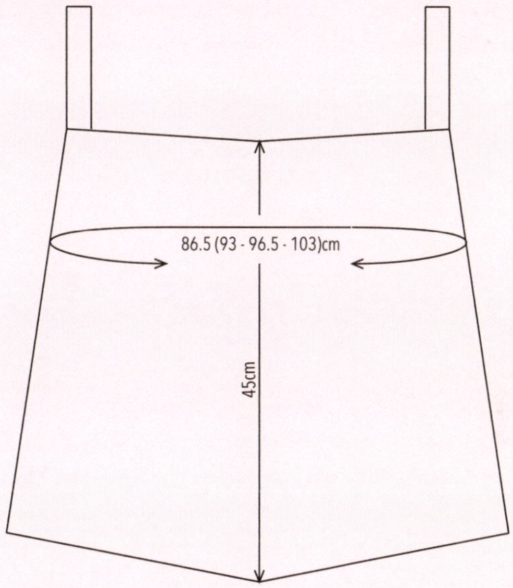

MATERIALS

Scheepjes Linen Soft (27% linen, 47% cotton, 26% acrylic, 50g/135m)
605 x 3 (3, 3, 4) balls
4.5mm crochet hook

MEASUREMENTS

To fit S (M, L, XL)
Finished bust 86.5 (93: 96.5: 103)cm (34.6 (37.2: 38.6: 41.2) in)
Finished length 45cm (18in) measured from centre neckline to centre bottom hem

TENSION/GAUGE

This pattern has a lot of positive ease.

SPECIAL ABBREVIATIONS

half dtr yoh twice, insert hook in next st, yoh, pull through st, (yoh, pull through 2 loops) twice, 2 loops remaining on hook
half tr yoh, insert hook into st indicated, yoh, pull through st, yoh, pull through 2 loops, 2 loops remaining on hook

PATTERN NOTES

This garment is worked top-down, the front and back are identical and worked separately. The two pieces are then joined at the sides and the straps are added. There are two different sets of instructions for the joining part, one set for sizes S and L, one set for sizes M and XL.
The only increases throughout the pattern will take place in the centre of the garment. The pattern is worked flat, turn after every row.

INSTRUCTIONS

52 (52: 62: 62) ch.

Row 1 (WS) 1dc in second ch from hook and in every ch to end. [51 (51: 61: 61) dc]
Row 2 (RS) Ch1 (does not count as st throughout), 1dc, (ch5, miss 4 sts, 1dc in next st) 10 (10: 12: 12) times.
Row 3 Ch4, 1dc in first ch-5 sp, (ch5, 1dc in next ch-5 sp) 4 (4: 5: 5) times, ch1, (2tr, ch2, 2tr) all in next dc, ch1, 1dc in next ch-5 sp, (ch5, 1dc in next ch-5 sp) 4 (4: 5: 5) times, ch3, 1tr in last dc.
Row 4 Ch1, 1dc in top of first tr, (ch1, (1tr, ch1, 1tr) in next dc, ch1, 1dc in next ch-5 sp) 4 (4: 5: 5) times, ch1, (1tr, ch1, 1tr) in next dc, ch1, (2tr, ch2, 2tr) in ch-2 sp, (ch1, (1tr, ch1, 1tr) in next dc, ch1, 1dc in next ch-5 sp) 4 (4: 5: 5) times, ch1, (1tr, ch1, 1tr) in next dc, ch1, 1dc in ch-4 sp.
Row 5 Ch4, 1dc in top ch-1 sp (i.e. between 2 tr), (ch5, 1dc in next top ch-1 sp) 4 (4: 5: 5) times, ch3, (2tr, ch2, 2tr) in ch-2 sp, ch3, 1dc in top ch-1 sp, (ch5, 1dc in next top ch-1 sp) 4 (4: 5: 5) times, ch3, 1tr in next dc.
Row 6 Ch1, 1dc in top of first tr, (ch5, 1dc in next ch-5 sp) 4 (4: 5: 5) times, ch5, 1dc in next ch-3 sp, ch2, (2tr, ch2, 2tr) in ch-2 sp, ch2, 1dc in next ch-3 sp, (ch5, 1dc in next ch-5 sp) 4 (4: 5: 5) times, ch5, 1dc in next ch-4 sp.
Row 7 Ch3, 1dtr in next ch-5 sp, (ch4, 1 half dtr in same ch-5 sp, 1 half dtr in next ch-5 sp, yoh and pull through all loops on hook) 4 (4: 5: 5) times, ch4, 1 half dtr in same ch-5 sp, 1 half tr in next ch-2 sp, yoh and pull through all loops on hook, ch2, (2tr, ch2, 2tr) in ch-2 sp, ch2, 1 half tr in next ch-2 sp, 1 half dtr in next ch-5 sp, yoh and pull through all loops on hook, (ch4, 1 half dtr in same ch-5 sp, 1 half dtr in next ch-5 sp, yoh and pull through all loops on hook) 4 (4: 5: 5) times, ch4, 1 half dtr in same ch-5 sp, 1 half dtr in next dc, yoh and pull through all loops on hook.
Row 8 Ch3, (5tr in next ch-5 sp) 5 (5: 6: 6) times, 1tr in next ch-2 sp, ch2, (2tr, ch2, 2tr) in ch-2 sp, ch2, 1tr in next ch-2 sp, (5tr in next ch-5 sp) 5 (5: 6: 6) times, 1tr in last dtr.
Row 9 Ch3, 1tr in next tr, 1 half tr in next tr, miss 1 st, 1 half tr in next tr, yoh and pull through all loops on hook, (ch3, 1 half tr in same tr, miss 3 sts, 1 half tr in next tr, yoh and pull through all loops on hook) 5 (5: 6: 6) times, ch3, 1 half tr in same tr, miss 1 st, 1 half tr in next tr, yoh and pull through all loops on hook, 1tr in next st (i.e. ch1 for sizes S-M, 1tr for sizes L-XL), ch2, (2tr, ch2, 2tr) in ch-2 sp, ch2, →

1tr in next st (i.e. ch-2 sp for sizes S-M, 1tr for sizes L-XL), 1 half tr in next tr, miss 1 st, 1 half tr in next tr, yoh and pull through all loops on hook, (ch3, 1 half tr in same tr, miss 3 sts, 1 half tr in next tr, yoh and pull through all loops on hook) 5 (5: 6: 6) times, ch3, 1 half tr in same tr, miss 1 st, 1 half tr in next tr, yoh and pull through all loops on hook, 1tr in each of next 2 sts.

Row 10 Ch3, 1tr in each of next 2 sts, (3tr in next ch-3 sp, 1tr in next st) 6 (6: 7: 7) times, 1tr in next st, ch2, (2tr, ch2, 2tr) in ch-2 sp, ch2, 1tr in each of next 2 sts, (3tr in next ch-3 sp, 1tr in next st) 6 (6: 7: 7) times, 1tr in each of next 2 sts.

Row 11 Ch4, miss 1 st, 1dc in next st, (ch5, miss 4 sts, 1dc in next st) 5 (5: 6: 6) times (last st will be a ch-sp for sizes L-XL), ch2, (2tr, ch2, 2tr) in ch-2 sp, ch2, 1dc in next st (first tr for sizes S-M, first ch-sp for sizes L-XL), (ch5, miss 4 sts, 1dc in next st) 5 (5: 6: 6) times, ch2, 1tr in last st.

Row 12 Ch1, 1dc in top of first tr, (ch5, 1dc in next ch-5 sp) 5 (5: 6: 6) times, ch3, 1tr in ch-2 sp, ch2, (2tr, ch2, 2tr) in ch-2 sp, ch2, 1tr in ch-2 sp, ch3, 1dc in next ch-5 sp, (ch5, 1dc in next ch-5 sp) 4 (4: 5: 5) times, ch5, 1dc in next ch-4 sp.

Rows 13 – 22 are essentially the same as **Rows 3 – 12** with minor differences. The rows are still written down in their entirety, but for your convenience the differences have been highlighted.

Row 13 Ch4, 1dc in first ch-5 sp, (ch5, 1dc in next ch-5 sp) 4 (4: 5: 5) times, **ch5, 1dc in next ch-3 sp, ch3,** (2tr, ch2, 2tr) in **next ch-2 sp, ch3,** 1dc in next **ch-3 sp,** (ch5, 1dc in next ch-5 sp) **5 (5: 6: 6) times**, ch3, 1tr in last dc.

Row 14 Ch1, 1dc in top of first tr, (ch1, (1tr, ch1, 1tr) in next dc, ch1, 1dc in next ch-5 sp) **5 (5: 6: 6) times**, ch1, (1tr, ch1, 1tr) in next dc, ch1, (2tr, ch2, 2tr) in ch-2 sp, (ch1, (1tr, ch1, 1tr) in next dc, ch1, 1dc in next ch-5 sp) **5 (5: 6: 6) times**, ch1, (1tr, ch1, 1tr) in next dc, ch1, 1dc in ch-4 sp.

Row 15 Ch4, 1dc in top ch-1 sp (between two tr), (ch5, 1dc in next top ch-1 sp) **5 (5: 6: 6) times**, ch3, (2tr, ch2, 2tr) in ch-2 sp, ch3, 1dc in top ch-1 sp, (ch5, 1dc in next top ch-1 sp) **5 (5: 6: 6) times**, ch3, 1tr in next dc.

Row 16 Ch1, 1dc in top of first tr, (ch5, 1dc in next ch-5 sp) **5 (5: 6: 6) times**, ch5, 1dc in next ch-3 sp, **ch3,** (2tr, ch2, 2tr) in ch-2 sp, **ch3,** 1dc in next ch-3 sp, (ch5, 1dc in next ch-5 sp) **5 (5: 6: 6) times**, ch5, 1dc in next ch-4 sp.

Row 17 Ch3, 1dtr in next ch-5 sp, (ch4, 1 half dtr in same ch-5 sp, 1 half dtr in next ch-5 sp, yoh and pull through all loops on hook) **5 (5: 6: 6) times**, ch4, 1 half dtr in same ch-5 sp, 1 half tr in next **ch-3 sp,** yoh and pull through all loops on hook, ch2, (2tr, ch2, 2tr) in ch-2 sp, ch2, 1 half tr in next **ch-3 sp,** 1 half dtr in next ch-5 sp, yoh and pull through all loops on hook, (ch4, 1 half dtr in same ch-5 sp, 1 half dtr in next ch-5 sp, yoh and pull through all loops on hook) **5 (5: 6: 6) times**, ch4, 1 half dtr in same ch-5 sp, 1 half dtr in next dc, yoh and pull through all loops on hook.

Row 18 Ch3, (5tr in next ch-5 sp) **6 (6: 7: 7) times**, 1tr in next ch-2 sp, ch2, (2tr, ch2, 2tr) in ch-2 sp, ch2, 1tr in next ch-2 sp, (5tr in next ch-5 sp) **6 (6: 7: 7) times**, 1tr in last dtr.

Row 19 Ch3, 1tr in next tr, 1 half tr in next tr, miss 1 st, 1half tr in next tr, yoh and pull through all loops on hook, (ch3, 1 half tr in same tr, miss 3 sts, 1 half tr in next tr, yoh and pull through all loops on hook) **6 (6: 7: 7) times**, ch3, 1 half tr in same tr, miss 1 st, 1 half tr in next tr, yoh and pull through all loops on hook, **1tr in next st, (Sizes L-XL only work 1tr in next st),** 1tr in next ch-2 sp, ch2, (2tr, ch2, 2tr) in ch-2 sp, ch2, 1tr in next ch-2 sp, **(Sizes L-XL only work 1tr in next st), 1tr in next st,** 1 half tr in next tr, miss 1 st, 1half tr in next tr, yoh and pull through all loops on hook, (ch3, 1 half tr in same tr, miss 3 sts, 1 half tr in next tr, yoh and pull through all loops on hook) **6, (6: 7: 7) times**, ch3, 1 half tr in same tr, miss 1 st, 1 half tr in next tr, yoh and pull through all loops on hook, 1 tr in each of next 2 sts.

Row 20 Ch3, 1tr in each of next 2 sts, (3tr in next ch-3 sp, 1tr in next st) **7 (7: 8: 8) times, 1tr in each of next (sizes S-M: 2 sts, sizes L-XL: 3 sts), 1 tr in ch-2 sp**, ch2, (2tr, ch2, 2tr) in ch-2 sp, ch2, **1tr in ch-2 sp**, 1tr in each of next **(sizes S-M: 3 sts, sizes L-XL: 4 sts)**, (3tr in next ch-3 sp, 1tr in next st) **7 (7: 8: 8) times**, 1tr in each of next 2 sts.

Row 21 Ch4, from base of ch sts, miss 1 st, 1dc in next st, (ch5, miss 4 sts, 1dc in next st) **6 (6: 7: 7) times, ch3,** (2tr, ch2, 2tr) in ch-2 sp, **ch3, 1dc in (second tr for sizes S-M, first tr for sizes L-XL),** (ch5, miss 4 sts, 1dc in next st) **6 (6: 7: 7) times**, ch2, 1tr in last st.

Row 22 Ch1, 1dc in top of first tr, (ch5, 1dc in next ch-5 sp) **6 (6: 7: 7) times**, ch3, 1tr in **ch-3 sp,** ch2, (2tr, ch2, 2tr) in ch-2 sp, ch2, 1tr in **ch-3 sp,** ch3, 1dc in next ch-5 sp, (ch5, 1dc in next ch-5 sp) **5 (5: 6: 6) times**, ch5, 1dc in next ch-4 sp.

Rows 23 – 32 are essentially another rep of **Rows 3 – 12**, the differences have been highlighted.

Row 23 Ch4, 1dc in first ch-5 sp, (ch5, 1dc in next ch-5 sp) **5 (5: 6: 6) times, ch5, 1dc in next ch-3 sp, ch4,** (2tr, ch2, 2tr) in next ch-2 sp, **ch4,** 1dc in next **ch-3 sp,** (ch5, 1dc in next ch-5 sp) **6 (6: 7: 7) times**, ch3, 1tr in last dc.

Row 24 Ch1, 1dc in top of first tr, (ch1, (1tr, ch1, 1tr) in next dc, ch1, 1dc in next ch-5 sp) **6 (6: 7: 7) times**, ch1, (1tr, ch1, 1tr) in next dc, **ch2,** (2tr, ch2, 2tr) in ch-2 sp, **ch2, (1tr, ch1, 1tr) in next dc, ch1, 1dc in next ch-5 sp,** (ch1, (1tr, ch1, 1tr) in next dc, ch1, 1dc in next ch-5 sp) **5 (5: 6: 6) times**, ch1, (1tr, ch1, 1tr) in next dc, ch1, 1dc in ch-4 sp.

Row 25 Ch4, 1dc in top ch-1 sp (between two tr), (ch5, 1dc in top ch-1 sp) **6 (6: 7: 7) times, ch4,** (2tr, ch2, 2tr) in ch-2 sp, **ch4,** 1dc in top ch-1 sp, (ch5, 1dc in next top ch-1 sp) **6 (6: 7: 7) times**, ch3, 1tr in next dc.

Row 26 Ch1, 1dc in top of first tr, (ch5, 1dc in next ch-5 sp) **6 (6: 7: 7) times**, ch5, 1dc in next **ch-4 sp, ch3,** (2tr, ch2, 2tr) in ch-2 sp, **ch3,** 1dc in next **ch-4 sp,** (ch5, 1dc in next ch-5 sp) **6 (6: 7: 7) times**, ch5, 1dc in next ch-4 sp.

Row 27 Ch3, 1dtr in next ch-5 sp, (ch4, 1 half dtr in same ch-5 sp, 1 half dtr in next ch-5 sp, yoh and pull through all loops on hook) **6 (6: 7: 7) times**, ch4, 1 half dtr in same ch-5 sp, 1 half tr in next **ch-3 sp,** yoh and pull through all loops on hook, ch2, (2tr, ch2, 2tr) in ch-2 sp, ch2, 1 half tr in next **ch-3 sp,** 1 half dtr in next ch-5 sp, yoh and pull through all loops on hook, (ch4, 1 half dtr in same ch-5 sp, 1 half dtr in next ch-5 sp, yoh and pull through all loops on hook) **6 (6: 7: 7) times**, ch4, 1 half dtr in same ch-5 sp, 1 half dtr in next dc, yoh and pull through all loops on hook.

Row 28 Ch3, (5tr in next ch-5 sp) **7 (7: 8: 8) times**, 1tr in next ch-2 sp, ch2, (2tr, ch2, 2tr) in ch-2 sp, ch2, 1tr in next ch-2 sp, (5tr in next ch-5 sp) **7 (7: 8: 8) times**, 1tr in last dtr.

Row 29 Ch3, 1tr in next tr, 1 half tr in next tr, miss 1 st, 1half tr in next tr, yoh and pull through all loops on hook, (ch3, 1 half tr in same tr, miss 3 sts, 1 half tr in next tr, yoh and pull through all loops on hook) **7 (7: 8: 8) times**, ch3, 1 half tr in same tr, miss 1 st, 1 half tr in next tr, yoh and pull through all loops on hook, **1 tr in each of next (sizes S-M: 2 sts; sizes L-XL: 3 sts)**, **1 tr in next ch-2 sp,** ch2, (2tr, ch2, 2tr) in ch-2 sp, ch2, **1tr in next ch-2 sp, 1 tr in each of next (sizes S-M: 2 sts; sizes L-XL: 3 sts)**, 1 half tr in next tr, miss 1 st, 1half tr in next tr, yoh and pull through all loops on hook, (ch3, 1 half tr in same tr, miss 3 sts, 1 half tr in next tr, yoh and pull through all loops on hook) 5 (5: 6: 6) times, ch3, 1 half tr in same tr, miss 1 st, 1 half tr in next tr, yoh and pull through all loops on hook, 1 tr in each of next 2 sts.

Row 30 Ch3, 1tr in each of next 2 sts, (3tr in next ch-3 sp, 1tr in next st) **8 (8: 9: 9) times**, **1tr in each of next (sizes S-M: 3 sts; sizes L-XL: 4 sts), 1 tr in ch-2 sp, ch1,** (2tr, ch2, 2tr) in ch-2 sp, **ch1, 1tr in ch-2 sp,** 1tr in each of next **(sizes S-M: 4 sts; sizes L-XL: 5 sts)**, (3tr in next ch-3 sp, 1tr in next st) **8 (8: 9: 9) times**, 1tr in each of next 2 sts.

Row 31 Ch4, from base of ch sts, miss 1 st, 1dc in next st, (ch5, miss 4 sts, 1dc in next st) **7 (7: 8: 8) times, ch3,** (2tr, ch2, 2tr) in ch-2 sp, **ch3,** 1dc in **(second tr for sizes S-M, third tr for sizes L-XL)**, (ch5, miss 4 sts, 1dc in next st) **7 (7: 8: 8) times**, ch2, 1tr in last st.

Row 32 Ch1, 1dc in top of first tr, (ch5, 1dc in next ch-5 sp) **7 (7: 8: 8) times**, ch3, 1tr in **ch-3 sp,** ch2, (2tr, ch2, 2tr) in ch-2 sp, ch2, 1tr in **ch-3 sp,** ch3, 1dc in next ch-5 sp, (ch5, 1dc in next ch-5 sp) **6 (6: 7: 7) times**, ch5, 1dc in next ch-4 sp.

Row 33 Ch4, 1dc in first ch-5 sp, (ch5, 1dc in next ch-5 sp) **6 (6: 7: 7) times, ch5, 1dc in next ch-3 sp, ch4,** (2tr, ch2, 2tr) in ch-2 sp, **ch4, 1dc in next ch-3 sp,** (ch5, 1dc in next ch-5 sp) **7 (7: 8: 8) times**, ch3, 1tr in last dc.

Row 34 Ch1, 1dc in top of first tr, (ch1, (1tr, ch1, 1tr) in next dc, ch1, 1dc in next ch-5 sp) **7 (7: 8: 8) times**, ch1, (1tr, ch1, 1tr) in next dc, ch1, **1dc in next ch-4 sp, ch1, (1tr, ch1, 1tr) in next ch-2 sp, ch1, 1dc in next ch-4 sp,** (ch1, (1tr, ch1, 1tr) in next dc, ch1, 1dc in next ch-5 sp) **7 (7: 8: 8) times**, ch1, (1tr, ch1, 1tr) in next dc, ch1, 1dc in ch-4 sp.

Rep Rows 1 – 34 for the other piece.
These two pieces will be the front and back of the top.

STRAPS

Row 1 Ch3, 2tr in first dc st of Row 1 of body, ch2, 1tr in same st, 1 half tr in same st, miss 1 st, 1 half tr in next st, yoh and pull through all loops on hook.

Row 2 Ch3, (2tr, ch2, 1tr) in ch-2 sp, 1 half tr in same ch-2 sp, 1 half tr in third ch of last row, yoh and pull through all loops on hook.

Rep Row 2 until strap reaches top of shoulder. For the garment shown here, Row 2 was repeated another 3 times.

Rep these instructions for the other side of the same piece, which will be the front.

SIZES S AND L ONLY

Front

Attach yarn to end of Row 34, 1dc, work (ch3, 1dc) along side of work. Space the dc sts with approx 1cm in between. Make note of how many dc you crochet until you reach the end.

Follow Strap instructions (see above).

Back

Attach yarn to other side of Row 34, 1dc. In between dc, work 1ss in ch-1 sp of front piece, joining the front and back together: After first dc, (ch1, 1ss to corresponding ch-3 sp, ch1, 1dc), repeat along the side until you want to start the armhole, which should be around 15cm starting from the top. From this point on work (ch3, 1dc) until you reach the other end.

Follow Strap instructions, break yarn but do not weave in ends yet. Repeat these instructions for the other side of the back, so that both sides are joined together. Use the ends attached to the straps to sew them together.

SIZES M AND XL ONLY

Front

Attach yarn to end of Row 34, (ch3, 2tr) in base of ch sts, work (ch1, 3tr) along side of the work, space the 3tr cl with approx. 1cm in between. Dc's at the beginning or end of rows are good places to work these stitches in. The garment shown here has 18 cl of 3tr in total along the edge, also counting the very first (ch3, 2tr).

Follow Strap instructions (see above).

Back

Crochet groups of 3tr along the side as for the front. But instead of ch1 between the shells, work 1ss to the ch-1 sp of the front piece, joining the front and back together:

Ch3, 2tr in base of ch sts, (1ss in corresponding ch-1 sp, 3tr) 11 times. From this point on, continue working ch1 between 3-tr shells, to make the armhole wide enough. Continue until you reach the other end, making sure this side has as many shells as the other side.

Follow Strap instructions, break yarn but do not weave in ends yet. Rep these instructions for the other side of the back, so that both sides are joined together. Then, use the ends attached to the straps to sew them together. ♦

CACTUS PUZZLE BALLS

BY
Dedri Uys
lookatwhatimade.net

MEASUREMENTS
ø 6.5cm (2.6in)
Each wedge measures 3cm (1.2in) from the point to the edge.

ABBREVIATIONS
See back cover flap

MATERIALS

Scheepjes Maxi Bonbon (100% mercerized cotton, 25g/140m)
1 ball each of:
Yarn A: 412 Forest Green
Yarn B: 411 Sweet Orange
Yarn C: 410 Rich Coral
Yarn D: 513 Spring Green
Yarn E: 397 Cyan
2mm crochet hook
Stuffing
Tapestry needle
Plant pots 6cm (2.4in) diameter

PATTERN NOTES

Each cactus consists of 3 rings or segments that have to be 'built' to form the cactus. The 'wedges' are made individually, but the 'lids' are made in 3 segments of 4 'lids' each.

INSTRUCTIONS

Wedges

(Make 12, using Yarn A for Puzzle Cactus 1 and Yarn D for Puzzle Cactus 2)
With Yarn A, ch2.

Row 1 3dc in second ch from hook, turn. [3 sts]
Row 2 Ch1 (doesn't count as st throughout), 2dc in each st, turn. [6 sts]
Row 3 Ch1, 2dc in st at base of ch, 1dc, (2dc in next st, 1dc) twice, turn. [9 sts]
Row 4 Ch1, 2dc in st at base of ch, 2dc, (2dc in next st, 2dc) twice, turn. [12 sts]
Row 5 Ch1, 2dc in st at base of ch, 3dc, (2dc in next st, 3dc) twice, turn. [15 sts]
Row 6 Ch1, 2dc in st at base of ch, 4dc, (2dc in next st, 4dc) twice, turn. [18 sts]
Row 7 Ch1, 2dc in st at base of ch, 5dc, (2dc in next st, 5dc) twice, turn. [21 sts]
Row 8 Ch1, 2dc in st at base of ch, 6dc, (2dc in next st, 6dc) twice, turn. [24 sts]
Row 9 Ch1, 2dc in st at base of ch, 7dc, (2dc in next st, 7dc) twice, turn. [27 sts]
Row 10 Ch1, 2dc in st at base of ch, 8dc, (2dc in next st, 8dc) twice, turn. [30 sts]
Row 11 Ch1, 2dc in st at base of ch, 9dc, (2dc in next st, 9dc) twice, turn. [33 sts]
Row 12 1ch, 2dc in st at base of ch, 10dc, (2dc in next st, 10dc) twice, turn. [36 sts

Close wedge Ch1, fold the semi-circle in half to form a quarter circle. Join the open sides of the resulting wedge together by working 10dc along the edge, working 1dc through both layers of each row except the first and last st. Fasten off and work away your tails by pulling them through the point of the wedge to use as part of the stuffing.

Wedge Lids

(Make 3, using Yarn A for Puzzle Cactus 1 and Yarn D for Puzzle Cactus 2)
Row 1 Ch2, 2dc in second ch from hook, turn. [2 sts]
Row 2 Ch1, 1dc in each st, turn. [2 sts]
Row 3 Ch1, 2dc in each st, turn. [4 sts]
Row 4 As Row 2. [4 sts]
Row 5 Ch1, 2dc in first st, 2dc, 2dc in last st, turn. [6 sts]
Row 6 As Row 2. [6 sts]
Row 7 Ch1, 2dc in first st, 4dc, 2dc in last st, turn. [8 sts]
Rows 8-10 As Row 2. [8 sts]
Row 11 Ch1, dc2tog, 4dc, dc2tog, turn. [6 sts]
Row 12 As Row 2. [6 sts]
Row 13 Ch1, dc2tog, 2dc, dc2tog, turn. [4 sts]
Row 14 As Row 2. [4 sts]
Row 15 Ch1, (dc2tog) twice, turn. [2 sts]
Row 16 As Row 2. [2 sts]
Row 17 Ch1, dc2tog, turn.
Rep Rows 1 – 17 **3 more times**. This will give a chain of 4 'lids'. On the fourth lid of the chain work ch1 and fasten off without working away yarn ends.

Assembly

Use Yarn A for Puzzle Cactus 1 and Yarn D for Puzzle Cactus 2.

Note: You will be attaching 4 'wedges' to each chain of 'lids', working up one side of the chain of 'lids' and down the other.

Insert hook through first ch st of a chain of 'lids' and through first st of the opening of one of the wedges, keeping the seam of the wedge to your right (left, if you are left-handed). Dc through both layers. Continue making a dc in each row and st of both layers until 18 dc have been worked into the first 'lid' and 'wedge'. Join next 'wedge' in same way and continue until one side of all 4 'wedges' has been joined to the chain of 'lids'.

Continue working around fourth 'wedge', stuffing as you go (tightly) and making 18 dc through both layers of 'wedge' and 'lid'. Do the same for 'wedges' 3, 2 and 1. When the last st of the first 'wedge' is reached, join to first st with a ss and fasten off. Use the yarn ends to join tips of first and last 'wedges' to each other to form a ring and work away yarn ends.

Rep this twice more so that you end up with 3 'rings'.

Building the Puzzle Ball
Use these rings to build the base for your cactus and then add embellishments as below.

Take 2 rings and slip half of one ring through the center of the other ring so that they form a cross. Take the third ring and slip it over the other two perpendicularly, placing each 'wedge' into one of the large 'gaps' created when you 'built' the first 2 rings. Make sure that all your 'wedges' are pointing inward and take a few seconds to tug the ball into a neat sphere.

This video link shows how to build the Puzzle Ball:
https://itsallinanutshell.com/2017/04/20/cactus-plants-in-yarn3/

PUZZLE CACTUS 1

Flower
With Yarn B make a magic ring.

Round 1 Ch1, 12tr in ring, join to flo of first tr with ss. [12 tr]
Round 2 (Ch8, ss) in flo of same st as ss, (ss, ch8, ss) in flo of rem 11 sts, fasten off, leaving a 10cm/4in yarn end. [12 ch-8 sp]
Round 3 Join Yarn C with ss in blo of any st in Round 1, ch1, (1dc, ch10, 1dc, ch10, 1dc) in same blo, (1dc, ch10, 1dc, ch10, 1dc) in blo of each rem st of Round 1, fasten off. [24 ch-10 sp and 48 dc]

Use yarn ends from Round 2 to sew flower to centre of any 'wedge lid' and work away yarn ends from Round 3.

PUZZLE CACTUS 2

Large Plant Part
(Worked in a spiral)
With Yarn D, make a magic ring.

Round 1 Ch1, 7dc in ring. [7 dc]
Round 2 2htr in each st. [14 htr]
Round 3 (2htr in next st, 1htr) 7 times. [21 htr]
Round 4 (2htr in next st, 2htr) 7 times. [28 htr]
Round 5 (2htr in next st, 3htr) 7 times. [35 htr]
Rounds 6-11 Htr in each st around. [35 htr]
Round 12 (Htr2tog, 3htr) 7 times. [28 htr]
Round 13 (Htr2tog, 2htr) 7 times. [21 htr]
Round 14 (Htr2tog, 1htr) 7 times. [14 htr]
Fasten off, stuff this part and sew it onto centre of any 'wedge lid'.

Small Plant Part
(Worked in a spiral)
With Yarn D, make a magic ring.

Round 1 Ch1, 7dc in ring. [7 dc]
Round 2 2htr in each st. [14 htr]
Round 3 (2htr in next st, 1htr) 7 times. [21 htr]
Rounds 4-6 Htr in each st around. [21 htr]
Round 7 (Htr2tog, 1htr) 7 times. [14 htr]
Round 8 (Htr2tog) 7 times. [7 htr]

Fasten off, stuff this part and sew it onto the side of Large Plant Part, placing it more towards the top than the bottom.

Flower
With Yarn E, make a magic ring.

Round 1 Ch1, 6dc in ring, ss to first dc to join. [6 dc]
Round 2 Ch4, ss in same st, (ss, ch4, ss) in each rem st.

Fasten off, leaving a 10cm (4in) yarn end. [6 ch-4 petals]
Using yarn ends, sew flower to first round of Small Plant Part above, weave in ends. ♦

AMAZON BLANKET

BY
Rachele Carmona
cypresstextiles.net

MEASUREMENTS
± 152 x 142cm
60.8in x 56.8in

ABBREVIATIONS
See back cover flap

MATERIALS

Scheepjes Softfun (60% cotton, 40% acrylic, 50g/140m)
Yarn A: 2516 x 3 balls
Yarn B: 2517 x 4 balls
Yarn C: 2470 x 1 ball
Yarn D: 2426 x 2 balls
Yarn E: 2491 x 1 ball
Yarn F: 2431 x 1 ball
Yarn G: 2531 x 2 balls
Yarn H: 2535 x 5 balls

Scheepjes Softfun Denim (60% cotton, 40% acrylic, 50g/140m)
Yarn I: 507 x 1 ball
Yarn J: 505 x 3 balls
Yarn K: 506 x 3 balls
Yarn L: 516 x 3 balls
Yarn M: 517 x 3 balls
Yarn N: 519 x 3 balls
4mm crochet hook

SPECIAL ABBREVIATIONS

beg dtr beginning double treble crochet: work 1dc, ch2, second ch counts as top of st - counts as first dtr of Round/Row
beg dtr4tog beginning double treble crochet 4 together: work beg dtr, 3dtr in indicated st/sp, leaving one loop behind each time, yoh, draw through all 4 loops on hook
beg tr beginning treble crochet: work 1dc, ch1, this ch counts as top of st - counts as first tr of Round/Row
beg tr4tog beginning treble crochet 4 together: work beg tr, 3tr in indicated st/sp, leaving one loop behind each time, yoh, draw through all 4 loops on hook
beg ttr beginning triple treble crochet: work 1dc, ch3, third ch counts as top of st - counts as first ttr of Round/Row
dec2tog decrease 1 st by working 2 tr together: make tr in next 2 sts indicated, leaving one loop behind each time, yoh, draw through all 3 loops on hook
dec3tog decrease 2 sts by working 3 tr together: make tr in next 3 sts indicated, leaving one loop behind each time, yoh, draw through all 4 loops on hook
MC main colour
split dec4tog decrease foll 4 sts together, missing centre decrease of previous Row at middle: *work tr in next 2 sts indicated, leaving one loop behind each time**, miss 1, rep from * to **, yoh, draw through all 5 loops on hook.

PATTERN NOTES

Three panels are worked first (see schematic for layout and colours), then whip stitched together to form blanket body. A small leaf edging is worked down the length on both sides of the blanket body, and granny squares are made from all colour remnants, then whip stitched onto the leaf edging in a vertical row on both sides. Once this is complete, a border is added around the entire piece. To keep a flat edge and minimize ruffling, this pattern does not contain any turning chains. See Special Abbreviations for instruction on beg st of Round/Row.

INSTRUCTIONS

Panel (make 3)

Flower Granny Square (make 9 for each panel)

Ch3, join with ss in first ch to make ring.

Round 1 In ring: Beg tr, 11tr, join with ss to beg tr. [12 tr]
Round 2 Beg dtr4tog, (ch2, dtr4tog) twice, *ch4, (dtr4tog, ch2) twice, dtr4tog; rep from * twice more, ch1, 1dtr in top of beg dtr4tog. [12 dtr4tog]
Round 3 (Beg tr, 3tr) around final dtr from previous Round, ch2, tr4tog in next ch-sp, ch1, tr4tog in next ch-sp, *ch2, 5tr in corner ch-sp, ch2, tr4tog in next ch-sp, ch1, tr4tog in next ch-sp; rep from * twice more, 1tr in first corner ch-sp, join with ss to beg tr. [8 tr4tog, 4 5-tr corners]
Round 4 (Beg tr, ch1, 1tr) all in next st, 1tr, 1htr, (2dc in next ch-sp, 1dc in tr4tog) twice, 2dc in next ch-sp, 1htr, 1tr, *(1tr, ch1, 1tr) in next st to make corner, 1tr, 1htr, (2dc in next ch-sp, 1dc in tr4tog) twice, 2dc in next ch-sp, 1htr, 1tr; rep from * twice more, join with ss to beg tr.
Round 5 (3dc in ch-sp, 1dc in next 14 sts) 4 times. [68 dc]

Half Flower Granny Square (make 2 per panel)

Ch3, join with ss in first ch to make ring.

Row 1 (WS) In ring: Beg tr, 7tr, turn. [8 tr]
Row 2 Beg ttr in first st, ch2, *(dtr4tog, ch2) twice, dtr4tog**, ch4, rep from * to **, ch2, ttr in final st, turn.
Row 3 Beg tr in first st, 2tr in ch-sp, *ch2, (tr4tog in ch-sp, ch2) twice**, 5tr in ch-sp, rep from * to **, ch2, 2tr in ch-sp, 1tr in final st, turn.
Row 4 (Beg dtr, ch1, 1tr) in first st, *1tr, 1htr, (2dc in next ch-sp, 1dc in tr4tog) twice, 2dc in next ch-sp, 1htr, 1tr**, (1tr, ch1, 1tr) in next st, rep from * to **, (1tr, ch1, 1dtr) in final st, turn.
Row 5 1dc in first and all foll st/sps to corner ch-sp, 3dc in corner, 1dc in all sts across, fasten off.

AMAZON BLANKET LAYOUT AND COLOURS

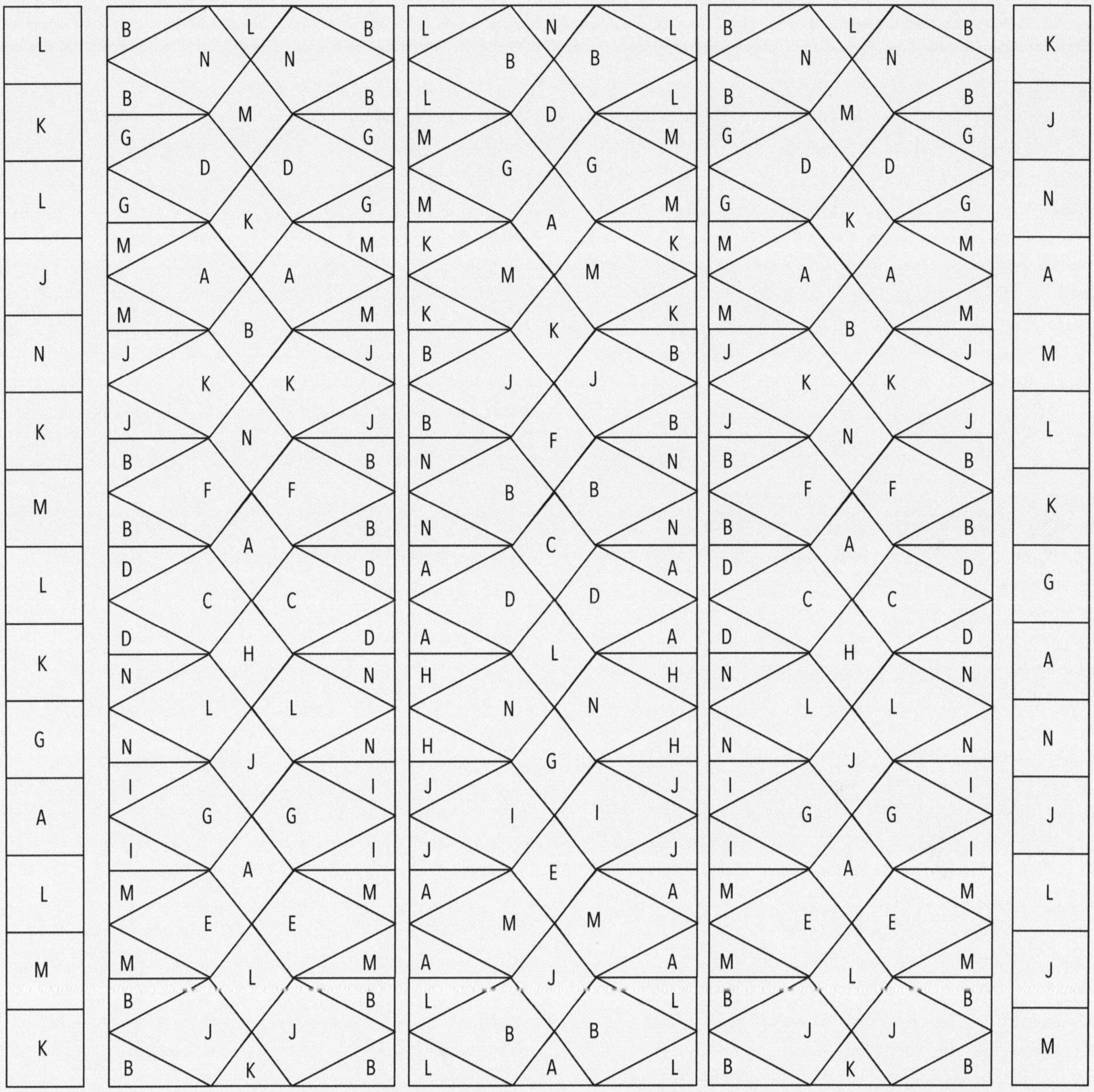

Leaf Spike (Joins Flower Granny Squares in diamond orientation)

Row 1 (RS) Pick up Flower Granny Square and with **RS** facing, join yarn with ss in corner dc, 1dc in same st and foll 16 sts, insert hook in next st, yoh, pull loop through, pick up Half Flower Granny Square and with **RS** facing, insert hook in corner dc, yoh, pull loop through, yoh, draw yarn through both loops on hook, 1dc in next 17 sts, turn.

Row 2 (Beg tr, 1tr) in first st, 1tr in next 14 sts, work split dec4tog, 1tr in next 14 sts, 2tr in final st, turn.

Row 3 Beg tr in first and foll 13 sts, work split dec4tog, 1tr in next 14 sts, turn.

Row 4 (Beg tr, 1tr) in first st, (miss 2 sts, 3tr in next st) 4 times, miss 3 sts, (3tr in next st, miss 2 sts) 4 times, 2tr in last st, turn.

Row 5 1dc in first st (does not count as st), 1tr in next st, (ch2, dec3tog) 4 times, ch1, (dec3tog, ch2) 4 times, dec2tog, turn.

Row 6 Beg tr in first st, (2tr in next ch-sp, 1tr) 3 times, work split dec4tog placing tr sts in ch-sps and missing two dec3tog, (1tr, 2tr in next ch-sp) 3 times, 1tr in last st, turn.

Row 7 Beg tr in first and foll 7 sts, work split dec4tog, 1tr in next 8 sts, turn.

Row 8 Beg dtr in first st, ch1, miss 1 st, (1dtr, ch1, miss 1 st) twice, *yoh twice, insert hook in next st, yoh, pull loop through, (yoh, draw through 2 loops on hook) twice (working in same st) **, miss 3 sts, rep from * to **, yoh, draw through all 3 loops on hook, (ch1, miss 1 st, 1dtr) 3 times, turn. →

Row 9 (Beg tr, 1tr) in first st, 1tr in next 4 sts, *yoh, insert hook in next ch-sp, yoh, pull loop through, yoh, draw through 2 loops on hook**, miss 1 st, rep from * to **, yoh, draw through all 3 loops on hook, 1tr in next 4 sts, 2tr in last st, turn.
Row 10 Beg tr in first and foll 3 sts, work split dec4tog, 1tr in next 4 sts, turn.
Row 11 (Beg tr, 1tr) in first st, 1tr, work split dec4tog, 1tr, 2tr in last st, turn.
Row 12 Beg tr in first st, work split dec4tog, 1tr in last st, turn.
Row 13 Beg tr in first st, dec2tog, fasten off.
Row 14 (Creates smooth edge on Leaf Spike) With **RS** facing, reattach yarn with ss in side post of first dc of Row 1, work 25dc evenly across to tip of Leaf Spike, (1dc, ch1, 1dc) in top of Row 13 to make Peak, work 25dc evenly down other side, ending in side post of final dc of Row 1, fasten off.

Work another Leaf Spike on opposite side, beg in first st of Half Flower Granny Square. Join remaining Flower Granny Squares in this same manner by working Leaf Spike on both sides. End by joining second Half Flower Granny Square.

Fill Triangle Gaps
First half of Triangle Gap
Row 1 Hold work with **RS** facing and join yarn with ss in second dc of Leaf Spike Peak, 1dc in same and foll 25 sts, turn.
Row 2 Miss first st, ss in next st, 1dc, 1htr, 1tr in next 20 sts, dec2tog, turn.
Row 3 Beg tr (does not count as st), dec2tog, 1tr in next 15 sts, 1htr, 1dc, ss, turn.
Row 4 Miss 1 st, ss, 1dc, 1htr, 1tr in next 11 sts, dec2tog, turn.
Row 5 Beg tr (does not count as st), dec2tog, 1tr in next 5 sts, 1htr, 1dc, ss, turn.
Row 6 Miss 1 st, ss, 1dc in next 5 sts, turn.
Row 7 1dc in first and foll 2 sts, ss, turn.
Row 8 Miss 1 st, beg tr, dec2tog, rotate to long side of triangle to make a clean edge, work 21dc evenly down edge, ending at bottom of Row 2, cut yarn, leaving long tail to whip stitch halves together if necessary to fill in Triangle Gap.

Second half of Triangle Gap
With **WS** facing, work as for First half of Triangle Gap, beg in first dc of Leaf Spike Peak. When Row 8 is complete, cut yarn, leaving a long tail if this triangle completes the triangle gap. Whip stitch the halves together, cut yarn, and weave in ends. Rep down the panel in this manner, filling all triangle gaps until the panel is a complete rectangle.

Edge Panel
Join MC (Yarn H) with ss in corner of Panel before a short side, *3dc in corner, dc 69 sts evenly across short side to corner, 3dc in corner, dc 247 sts evenly down long side to corner; rep from * once, join with ss to first dc, fasten off.
Make 2 more panels the same.
When 3 Panels are complete, whip stitch together using MC.

Leaf Side Edging
Row 1 With **RS** facing, join MC with ss in corner of work before a long side, dc in each st across, turn.
Row 2 (Beg tr, 1tr) in first st, (miss 2 sts, 3tr in next st) across until 3 sts rem, miss 2 sts, 2tr in last st, turn.
Row 3 1dc in first st (does not count as st), 1tr, (ch2, dec3tog) across until 2 sts rem, ch2, dec2tog, turn.
Row 4 1dc in first st, 3dc in each ch-sp across, 1dc in last st, turn.
Row 5 1dc in each st across, fasten off.
Repeat on opposite side.

Granny Square Sides
Using remnants of yarn colours, make 28 Flower Granny Squares. Edge all 28 squares in MC as follows: join MC with ss in any corner, (3dc in corner, dc across to corner) 4 times, join with ss in first dc, fasten off.

Using MC, whip stitch 14 squares together to form a long strip.

Whip stitch those 2 strips on both long sides of piece, using about 18 sts per square.

Border
Round 1 With **RS** facing, join MC with ss in any corner, (3dc in corner, dc across to corner) 4 times, join with ss in first dc.
Round 2 (Beg tr, 2tr, ch1, picot 3, ch1, 3tr) all in corner dc, ** *miss 4 sts, (3tr, ch1, picot 3, ch1, 3tr) in next st; rep from * across to corner, (3tr, ch1, picot 3, ch1, 3tr) in corner; rep from ** around all sides to first corner, join with ss in beg tr, fasten off and weave in all ends. ♦

STAR FRUIT BLANKET

BY
Atty van Norel
atty-s.blogspot.com

MEASUREMENTS
110 x 155cm
(44in x 62in)

ABBREVIATIONS
See back cover flap

MATERIALS
Scheepjes Catona Denim (100% cotton, 50g/125m)
Yarn A: 131 x 2 balls
Yarn B: 124 x 4 balls
Yarn C1: 166 x 5 balls
Yarn C2: 170 x 5 balls
5mm crochet hook

PATTERN NOTES
Make a total of 140 motifs, working 70 with Round 3 worked in Yarn C1 and also 70 with Round 3 worked in Yarn C2. Join the motifs using the join-as-you-go method described below. Make a full motif first, then join from the second motif onwards. The blanket is made up of 10 rows of 14 motifs each.

INSTRUCTIONS
Motif
With Yarn A, ch4, ss to first ch to join.

Round 1 Ch2 (counts as first tr), 11tr in ring, ss in top of 2 ch to join. Fasten off Yarn A.
Round 2 Join Yarn B, ch2 (counts as first tr), 1tr in same st, *2tr in next st, (1tr, ch5, 1tr) in next st, 2tr in next st; rep from * twice more, 2tr in next st, (1tr, ch5, 1tr) in next st, ss in top of 2 ch to join. Fasten off Yarn B.
Round 3 Join either Yarn C1 or C2 with a ss between third and fourth st either side of ch-sp, *ch7, ss in same st, (7tr, 1dtr, ch3, 1dtr, 7tr) in ch-5 sp, ss between third and fourth st from ch-sp; rep from * 3 times, ss in first ss to join.

Join-as-you-go method
Remove hook from your work in round 3 before every second ch in the corner, put hook through the corner of a finished square, pick up the loop from the square you are working on, pull through and crochet the second ch (which becomes more of a ss now). Continue according round 3 of pattern, take the hook out before every fourth ch from the loop in the middle, put your hook through the loop from the finished square, pick up the loop from the square you are working on, pull through and crochet the fourth ch (which also becomes more of a ss). Continue according the pattern and finish the square.

TO FINISH
Weave in all ends.

STAR FRUIT MOTIF

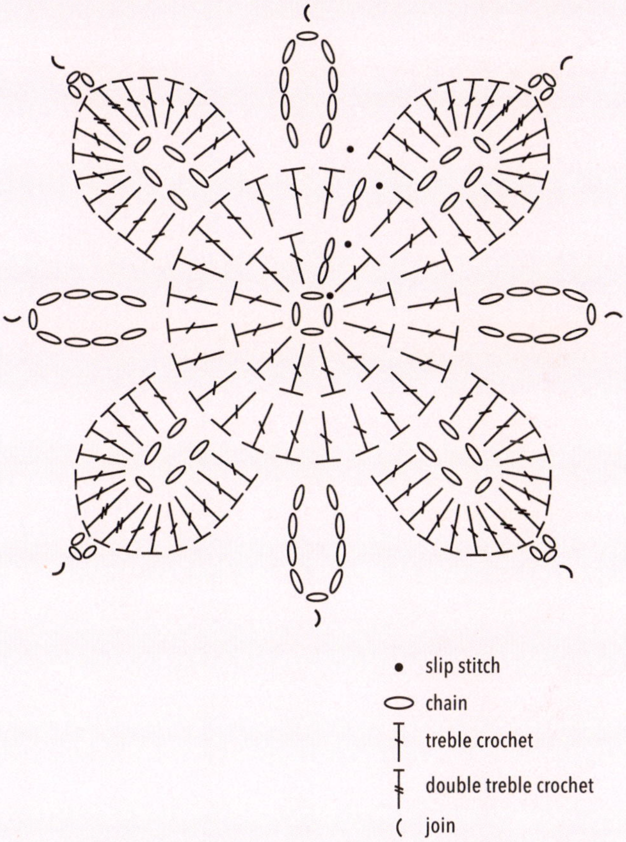

TROPICAL FLOWER POUF

BY
Tatsiana Kupryianchyk
lillabjorncrochet.com

MEASUREMENTS
ø 50cm (20in)
Hight 40cm (16in)

ABBREVIATIONS
See back cover flap

MATERIALS
Scheepjes Bloom (100% cotton 50g/80m)
Yarn A: 412 Light Fern x 5 balls
Yarn B: 410 Chrysanthemum x 5 balls
Yarn C: 408 Geranium x 4 balls
Yarn D: 419 Forget-Me-Not x 5 balls
Yarn E: 414 Sun Flower x 4 balls
4.5mm crochet hook
2 handles x 30cm (12in) long Opry art. 99577 (black)
Filling

TENSION/GAUGE
18 sts and 10 rows to 10 x 10cm over treble crochet using 4.5mm hook
Diameter of mandala after round 4 is 10cm (4in)

SPECIAL ABBREVIATION
pc (popcorn) work 5tr in next st, remove hook from stitch and insert from front to back in top of first tr made, pick up the dropped stitch and pull through, work ch1. This ch1 immediately worked after the popcorn does not count as a stitch, which means that the next stitch you have to work is always made in the first stitch after this ch1.

PATTERN NOTES
The pouf consist of the following parts: two mandalas, one for the top and one for the bottom, a side piece and 4 small rectangles to attach the handles. The yarn colours for the second mandala are given in brackets. Always work popcorn (pc) in next available stitch.

INSTRUCTIONS
Mandala (make two)
With Yarn A (B), make a magic ring.

Round 1 (RS) Ch2 (does not count as st here and throughout), 12tr in ring, ss in top of first tr. [12 tr]
Round 2 Ch2, 2tr in st at base of ch, 2tr in each st around, ss in first tr. [24 tr]
Fasten off.

Round 3 Join Yarn B (D) with 1tr in second tr of any 2-tr gr (this 2-tr gr is referred to below as an increase), 2tr in next st, (1tr, 2tr in next st) 11 times, ss to first tr. [36 tr]
Round 4 Ch2, 2tr in same st at base of ch, 1tr, 1pc, (2tr in next st, 1tr, 1pc) 11 times, ss in first tr. [36 tr, 12 pc]
Fasten off.
Round 5 Join Yarn C (E) with 1tr in any pc, 1tr in same st at base of ch, 1tr, 1pc, 1tr, (2tr in top of pc, 1tr, 1pc, 1tr) 11 times, ss in first tr. [48 tr, 12 pc]
Round 6 Ch2, 1tr in same st at base of ch, 1pc, 1tr, 2tr in top of pc, 1tr, (1tr, 1pc, 1tr, 2tr in top of pc, 1tr) 11 times, ss to first tr. [60 tr, 12 pc]
Round 7 Ch2, 1tr in same st at base of ch, 2tr in top of pc, 2tr, 1pc, 1tr, (1tr, 2tr in top of pc, 2tr, 1pc, 1tr) 11 times, ss to first tr. [72 tr, 12 pc]
Fasten off.

Round 8 Join Yarn D (A) with 1tr in any pc, 1tr, 1pc, 1tr, 2tr in next st, 1pc, 1tr, (2tr, 1pc, 1tr, 2tr in next st, 1pc, 1tr) 11 times, ss to first tr. [72 tr, 24 pc]
Round 9 Ch2, 1pc in same st at base of ch, 3tr, (1pc, 3tr) 23 times, ss to first pc. [72 tr, 24 pc]
Round 10 Ch2, 2tr in same st at base of ch, 1tr, 1pc, 3tr, 1pc, 1tr, (2tr in next pc, 1tr, 1pc, 3tr, 1pc, 1tr) 11 times, ss to first tr. [84 tr, 24 pc]
Fasten off.

Round 11 Join Yarn E (C) with 1tr in any pc before an inc, 2tr, 1pc, 1tr, 2tr in next pc, 1tr, 1pc, 1tr, (3tr, 1pc, 1tr, 2tr in next pc, 1tr, 1pc, 1tr) 11 times, ss to first tr. [96 tr, 24 pc]
Round 12 Ch2, 1tr in same st at base of ch, 1pc, 4tr, 1pc, 1tr, 2tr in next pc, 1tr, (1tr, 1pc, 4tr, 1pc, 1tr, 2tr in next pc, 1tr) 11 times, ss to first tr. [108 tr, 24 pc]
Round 13 Ch2, 1tr in same st at base of ch, 2tr in next pc, 1tr, 1pc, 5tr, 1pc, 1tr, (1tr, 2tr in next pc, 1tr, 1pc, 5tr, 1pc, 1tr) 11 times, ss to first tr. [120 tr, 24 pc]
Fasten off.

Round 14 Join Yarn B (D) with 1tr in any pc after an inc, 5tr, 2tr in next pc, 5tr, (6tr, 2tr in next pc, 5tr) 11 times, ss to first tr. [156 tr]
Fasten off.

Round 15 Join Yarn A (B) with 1dc in second tr of any increase, 3dc, miss 2 sts, 7dtr in next st, miss 2 sts, 4dc, (4dc, miss 2 sts, 7dtr in next st, miss 2 sts, 4dc) 11 times, ss to first dc. [96 dc, 84 dtr]
Round 16 Ch1 (doesn't count as st here and throughout), 1dc in same st at base of ch, 1dc, miss 2 sts, 3tr, 7tr in next st, 3tr, miss 2 sts, 2dc, (2dc, miss 2 sts, 3tr, 7tr in next st, 3tr, miss 2 sts, 2dc) 11 times, ss to first dc. [48 dc, 156 tr]
Fasten off.

Round 17 Join Yarn D (A) with 1dc in second dc of any group of 4 dc, 1dc, miss 1 st, 6tr, 5tr in next st, 6tr, miss 1 st, (2dc, miss 1 st, 6tr, 5tr in next st, 6tr, miss 1 st) 11 times, ss to first dc. [24 dc, 204 tr]
Fasten off.

Round 18 Join Yarn B (D) with 1dc in tenth tr of any group of 17 tr, 1dc, 2htr, 2tr, 6dtr, 2tr, 2htr, 3dc, (2dc, 2htr, 2tr, 6dtr, 2tr, 2htr, 3dc) 11 times, ss to first dc. [228 sts]
Round 19 Ch1, 1dc in same st at base of ch, 1dc, 2htr, 10tr, 2htr, 3dc, (2dc, 2htr, 10tr, 2htr, 3dc) 11 times, ss to first dc. [228 sts]
Fasten off.

Round 20 Join Yarn C (E) with 1dc in second dc of any group of 5 dc, 2dc, miss 3 sts, 7dtr in next st, miss 2 sts, 3dc, miss 3 sts, 7dtr in next st, miss 3 sts, (3dc, miss 3 sts, 7dtr in next st, miss 2 sts, 3dc, miss 3 sts, 7dtr in next st, miss 3 sts) 11 times, ss to first dc. [72 dc, 168 dtr]
Fasten off.

Round 21 Join Yarn D (A) with 1dc in second dc of any group of 3 dc, miss 1 st, 3tr, 5tr in next st, 3tr, miss 1 st, (1dc, miss 1 st, 3tr, 5tr in next st, 3tr, miss 1 st) 23 times, ss to first dc. [24 dc, 264 tr]
Fasten off.

Round 22 Join Yarn A (B) with 1dc in fifth tr of any group of 11 tr, 2dc, 1htr, 2tr, dtr3tog over the next 3 st, 2tr, 1htr, (3dc, 1htr, 2tr, dtr3tog over the next 3 st, 2tr, 1htr) 23 times, ss to first dc. [240 sts]

Round 23 Ch2, 1tr in same st at base of ch, 10tr, 2tr in next st, 8tr, (11tr, 2tr in next st, 8tr) 11 times, ss to first tr. [252 sts]
Fasten off and weave in ends.
Block to measurements.

SIDE

The side is worked in the round with stripes of 4 rows in each colour (i.e. 10 x 4-row stripes = 40 rows in total).

Stripes 1 and 6: Yarn D
Stripes 2 and 7: Yarn E
Stripes 3 and 8: Yarn C
Stripes 4 and 9: Yarn A
Stripes 5 and 10: Yarn B

Stripe 1

Round 1 Join Yarn D with 1tr blo in any st on last round of Mandala 2, 1tr blo in each st around, ss to first tr. [252 tr blo]
Rounds 2-4 Ch2, 1tr in same st at base of ch, 1tr in each st around, ss to first tr. [252 tr]
Fasten off

Rep Rounds 1-4 for each stripe but working Round 1 through both loops.
Weave in ends.

TO FINISH

Rectangle (make 4)

With Yarn B, ch6.

Row 1 1dc in second st from hook, 1dc in each st to end, turn. [5 dc]
Rows 2-8 Ch1 (does not count as st), 1dc in first st, 1dc in each st to end, turn.
Fasten off leaving a tail of approx. 20cm (8in) to sew to side of pouf.

Wear each rectangle on the ring of the handle, fold rectangle, centre handle on side of pouf between Rounds 5 and 6 and sew both rectangles using yarn tails.
Attach second handle in the same way.
Weave in ends.

Stuff pouf firmly and attach Mandala 1 on the top with "flat zipper method" using Yarn A:
Place Mandala on the top of the stuffed pouf **RS** facing. Insert hook from front to back through blo of any st of last Round of the Mandala. Insert hook from front to back through blo of any st of last Round on side, yoh and draw yarn through all 3 loops on hook. Continue joining in this way with ss in blo of each st around, ss to top of first ss.
Fasten off and weave tail in. ♦

WALL-HANGING FRUIT

BY
Jellina Verhoeff
jellina-creations.nl

MEASUREMENTS
90 x 102cm
(36in x 40in)

ABBREVIATIONS
See back cover flap

MATERIALS
Scheepjes Catona (100% mercerized cotton, 50g/125m)
Amethyst (240)
Shadow Purple (394)
Light Orchid (226)
Sweet Orange (411)
Yellow Gold (208)
Rich Opal (410)
Watermelon (252)
Rosewood (258)
Scarlet (192)
Dark Teal (401)
Tropic (253)
Chrystalline (385)
Apple Green (389)
Sage Green (212)
Parrot Green (241)
7 x 50g balls in Tyrian Purple (128)
2.5mm crochet hook
Tapestry needle
2 Broomsticks
2 Steel screw hooks
Crochet i-cord/chain 130cm (50in)

PATTERN NOTES
This wall hanging is composed of 5 different motifs, which are sewn together.
Chain at start of each Row does not count as a stitch.
Turn at end of each Row.

INSTRUCTIONS
MOTIF A Work 90 motifs - 6 motifs in each of the 15 contrast colours, do not work any in Tyrian Purple (128).
Leaving a 50cm tail, work ch50.

Row 1 1dc in second ch from hook, 22dc, dc3tog, 23dc. [47 dc]
Row 2 Ch1, 1dc in second dc from hook, 46dc.
Row 3 Ch1, 1dc in second dc from hook, 20dc, dc3tog, 21dc. [43 dc]
Row 4 Ch1, 1dc in second dc from hook, 42dc.
Row 5 Ch1, 1dc in second dc from hook, 18dc, dc3tog, 19dc. [39 dc]
Row 6 Ch1, 1dc in second dc from hook, 38dc.
Row 7 Ch1, 1dc in second dc from hook, 16dc, dc3tog, 17dc. [35 dc]
Row 8 Ch1, 1dc in second dc from hook, 34dc.
Row 9 Ch1, 1dc in second dc from hook, 14dc, dc3tog, 15dc. [31 dc]
Row 10 Ch1, 1dc in second dc from hook, 30dc.
Row 11 Ch1, 1dc in second dc from hook, 12dc, dc3tog, 13dc. [27 dc]
Row 12 Ch1, 1dc in second dc from hook, 26dc.
Fasten off, leaving a 50cm tail.

MOTIF B Work 24 in Tyrian Purple (128)
*Leaving a 35cm tail, work ch14.

Row 1 1dc in second ch from hook, dc in each ch to end. [13 dc]
Row 2 Ch1, 2dc in first dc, 12 dc. [14 dc]
Row 3 Ch1, 2dc in first dc, 13dc. [15 dc]
Rep last row 9 more times. [24 dc]**

Row 13 Ch1, 24dc.
Row 14 Ch1, dc2tog, 22dc. [23 dc]
Row 15 Ch1, dc2tog, 21dc. [22 dc]
Rep last row 9 more times. [13 dc]
Fasten off, leaving a 35cm tail.

MOTIF C Work 12 in Tyrian Purple (128)
Work as for Motif B from * to **.
MOTIF D Work 19 in Tyrian Purple (128)
*Leaving a 35cm tail, work ch25.

Row 1 2dc in second ch from hook, 23dc. [25 dc]
Row 2 Ch1, 2dc in first dc, 24dc. [26 dc]
Rep last row 4 more times. [30 dc]**

Row 7 Ch1, dc2tog, 28dc. [29 dc]
Rep last row 5 more times. [24 dc]
Fasten off, leaving a 35cm tail.

MOTIF E Work 2 in Tyrian Purple (128)
Work as for Motif D from * to **.

TO FINISH
Sew motifs together using an whip stitch. Pick up just a tiny amount of thread with each stitch, so the seam is almost invisible. Use the schematic for the correct placement of motifs. Motif D and E must be folded, these will form hanger loops.
Weave in all ends. Pull the broomstick through the loops. Screw the hooks in the broomstick. Attach the i-cord or chain to the hooks to hang.

WALL-HANGING FRUIT LAYOUT AND COLOURS

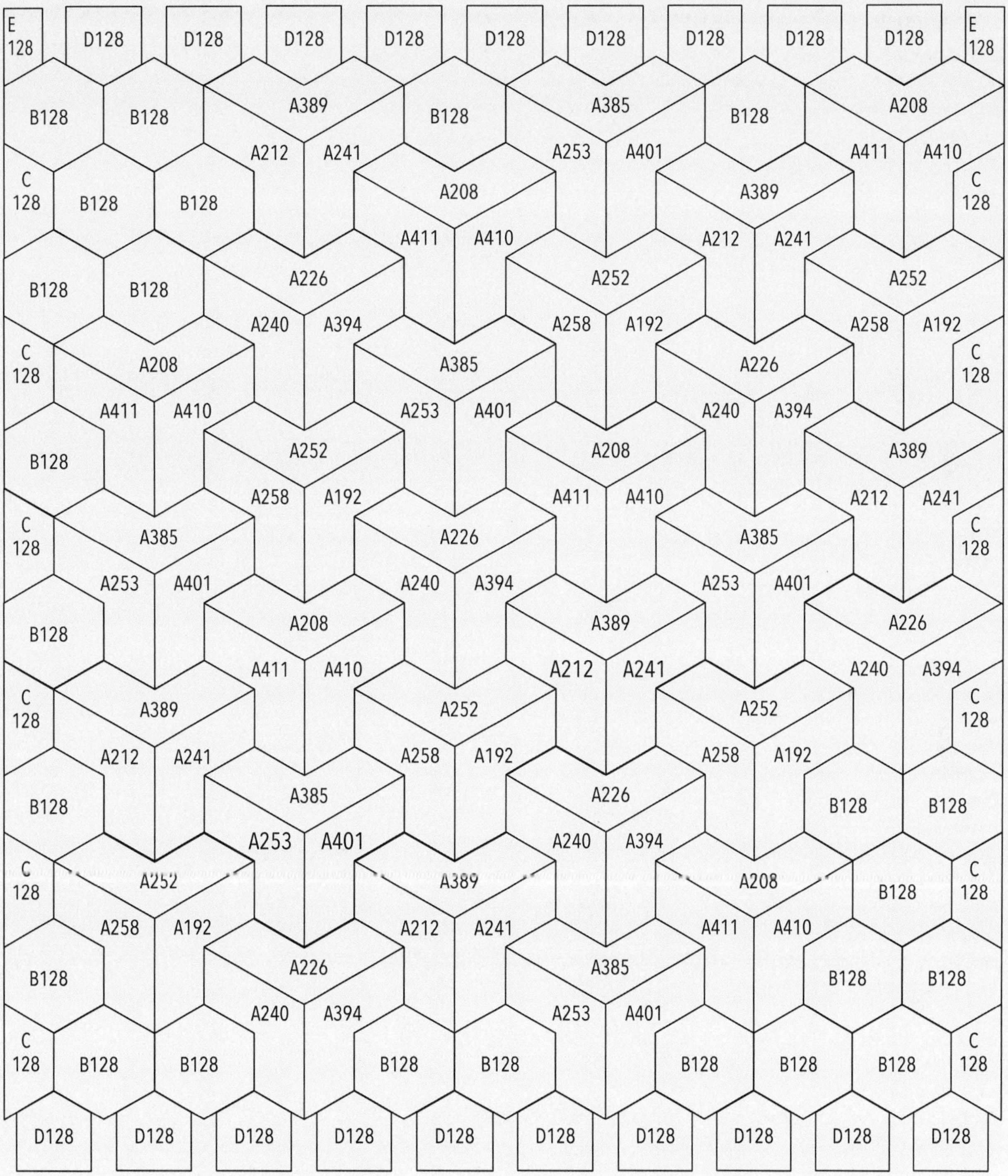

PINEAPPLE GARLAND

BY
Nerissa Muijs
missneriss.com

MEASUREMENTS
1 pineapple = 17 x 9cm (6.8in x 3.6in)

ABBREVIATIONS
See back cover flap

MATERIALS

Scheepjes Softfun Denim (60% cotton, 40% acrylic, 50g/140m)
520 x 1 ball
Scheepjes Softfun (60% cotton, 40% acrylic, 50g/140m)
2517 x 1 ball
4m x 5mm wide green ribbon
15cm x 20cm green pipe cleaners
4mm crochet hook

PATTERN NOTES

The body of the pineapples and the leaves are made in two separate pieces and then sewn together. Both items are worked back and forth in rows. The leaves are crocheted around the pipe cleaners, which can then be adjusted for shape.

INSTRUCTIONS

Pineapple (make 15)

Ch4, ss to fourth ch to make a ring.

Row 1 (RS) ch1, 9dc in ring, ss to join, turn.
Row 2 (WS) ch1, 2tr in same st, ch2, miss 2 dc, 2tr in next st, turn.
Row 3 Ch1, 2tr in first st, ch2, miss 1 tr, 7tr in ch-sp, ch2, miss 1 tr, 2tr in last st, turn.
Row 4 Ss in first st, (1dc, 2tr) in next st, ch2, (1tr in next tr, ch1) 6 times, 1tr in next st, ch2, 2tr in next tr, turn.
Row 5 Ss in first st, (1dc, 2tr) in next st, ch2, miss 1 ch and 1 tr, 1dc in next ch-sp, (ch3, 1dc in next ch-sp) 5 times, ch2, miss 1 tr and 1 ch, 2tr in next st, turn.
Row 6 Ss in first st, (1dc, 2tr) in next st, ch2, miss 1 ch and 1 dc, 1dc in next ch-sp, (ch3, 1dc in next ch-sp) 4 times, ch2, miss 1 dc and 1 ch, 2tr in next st, turn.
Row 7 Ss in first st, (1dc, 2tr) in next st, ch2, miss 1 ch and 1 dc, 1dc in next ch-sp, (ch3, 1dc in next ch-sp) 3 times, ch2, miss 1 dc and 1 ch, 2tr in next st, turn.
Row 8 Ss in first st, (1dc, 2tr) in next st, ch2, miss 1 ch and 1 dc, 1dc in next ch-sp, (ch3, 1dc in next ch-sp) twice, ch2, miss 1 dc and 1 ch, 2tr in next st, turn.
Row 9 Ss in first st, (1dc, 2tr) in next st, ch2, miss 1 ch and 1 dc, 1dc in next ch-sp, ch3, 1dc in next ch-sp, ch2, miss 1 dc and 1 ch, 2tr in next st, turn.
Row 10 Ss in first st, tr4tog inserting hook in next tr, next 2 dc and following tr.

Fasten off and weave in ends.

Leaves (make 15)

Make 15 13cm and 6cm lengths of pipe cleaners. Fold 13cm pieces in half and attach 6cm piece to the middle with a twist.

Row 1 Starting in the centre and working towards one end work 1dc, 1htr, 4tr, 4htr, 1dc, 1ch, turn work back down other side of pipe cleaner working 1dc, 4htr, 4tr, htr, 1dc, ss around centre point of pipe cleaner.

Rep Row 1 on each stem, fasten off leaving a tail to attach to the pineapple.

TO FINISH

Attach leaves to ring at top of pineapples and weave in ends. Thread ribbon through the leaves above join, taking care to check the balance of the pineapples. If the ribbon is threaded too low, the leaves will be top heavy and will not hang straight down. Space the pineapples evenly, leaving 1 metre at each end. ♦

BIRDS OF PARADISE SHAWL

BY
Bernadette Ambergen
berniolie.com

MEASUREMENTS
195 x 50cm
(78in x 20in)
Measured after blocking

ABBREVIATIONS
See back cover flap

MATERIALS

Scheepjes Cotton 8 (100% cotton, 50g/170m)

Colourway with main colour white:	Shades used in alternative colourway:
Yarn A: 502 x 3 balls	Yarn A: 700 x 3 balls
1 ball each of:	1 ball each of:
Yarn B: 719	716
Yarn C: 663	712
Yarn D: 529	713
Yarn E: 519	510
Yarn F: 665	551
Yarn G: 718	717
Yarn H: 726	654
Yarn I: 517	563
Yarn J: 563	720
Yarn K: 720	661

4mm crochet hook

TENSION/GAUGE

17tr and 10 rows to 10x10cm over treble crochet using 4mm hook

PATTERN NOTES

Instructions are the same for both shawls. Turn at end of each row unless otherwise stated. Work coloured stripes in the following order: B, A, C, A, D, A, E, A, F, A, G, A, H, A, I, A, J, A, K, A, K, A, J, A, I, A, H, A, G, A, F, A, E, A, D, A, C, A, B, A.

INSTRUCTIONS

With Yarn B and 4mm hook work ch314.

Row 1 1dc in second ch from hook, (ch3, miss 3 ch, 1dc in next ch) to end, turn.
Row 2 Ch3, 3tr in ch-3 sp, (ch1, 3tr in next ch-3 sp) to last st, 1tr in last dc, turn.
Row 3 Ch1, 1dc in first tr, ch3, miss 3 tr, 1dc in ch-sp, (ch3, 1dc in next ch-sp) to last 3 sts, ch3, miss 3 tr, 1dc in third of 3 ch, turn.
Row 4 As Row 2.
Row 5 As Row 3.
Fasten off B, join Yarn A.
Row 6 As Row 2.
Row 7 As Row 3, do not turn.
Fasten off. Rotate work 90 degrees. Join Yarn C in last dc worked and continue to work along side of rows as foll:
Row 8 ch3, (3tr in next tr, ch1) twice, 3tr, 1tr in first ch, turn.
Row 9 Ch1, 1dc in first tr, ch3, 1dc in ch-sp, (ch3, 1dc in next ch-sp), ch3, 1dc in third of 3 ch, turn.
Row 10 Ch3, 3tr in ch-3 sp, (ch1, 3tr in next ch-3 sp) twice, 1tr in last dc, turn.
Row 11 Ch1 (does not count as st), 1dc in first tr, (ch3, 1dc in next ch-sp) twice, ch3, 1dc in third of 3 ch, turn.
Fasten off. Join Yarn A.
Row 12 As Row 10.
Row 13 As Row 11, do not turn.
**Fasten off. Rotate work 90 degrees. Join Yarn D in last dc worked and continue along side of rows as foll:
Row 14 Ch3, (3tr in next tr, ch1) 3 times, (3tr in next tr, ch1) across, 3tr in ch-3 sp, 1tr in last dc, turn.
Row 15 Ch1, 1dc in first tr, (ch3, 1dc in next ch-sp) to end, ch3, 1dc in third of 3 ch, turn.
Row 16 Ch3, (3tr in ch-3 sp, ch1) to last ch-3 sp, 3tr in ch-3 sp, 1tr in last dc, turn.
Row 17 Ch1, 1dc in first tr, (ch3, 1dc in next ch-sp) to end, ch3, 1dc in third of 3 ch, turn.
Fasten off. Join Yarn A.
Row 18 As Row 16.
Row 19 As Row 17, do not turn.
Rep from ** a further 17 times working stripe sections in order given.
Weave in all ends and block to size.

BIRDS OF PARADISE SHAWL LAYOUT

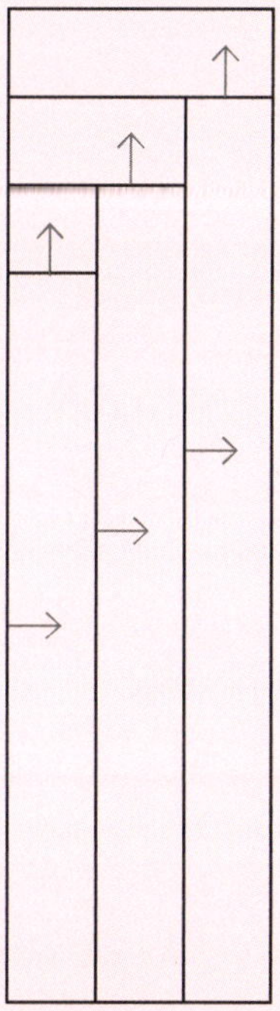

CLUB TROPICANA BAG

BY
Esther de Beer
happyinred.blogspot.nl

MEASUREMENTS
45 x 44cm
(18in x 17.5in)

ABBREVIATIONS
See back cover flap

MATERIALS

Tissu de Marie (art. 96074, 100% polyester):
0.5m x 1.5m of each: Purple (no. 4), Pink (no. 1)
Tissu de Marie Batik (art. 706020, 100% cotton):
0.5m x 1.5m of no. 12
KnitPro bag handles white (art. K10884)
2 metres off-white shoelace 3mm (art. 650010, colour 638)
Big wooden button (art. 2552-40)
Fusible interfacing
Sewing machine
Matching thread
Pins
Scissors
Tailor's chalk
Iron
Ironing board
Safety pin

PATTERN NOTES

All seam allowances are 1cm, unless otherwise stated.

INSTRUCTIONS

Preparing the fabric

1 Print the pattern pieces at 100% and cut as follows:
Template A: Cut 2 pieces in Purple, 2 in interfacing
Template B: Cut 2 pieces in Pink, 2 in interfacing
Template C: Cut 2 pieces in Batik, 2 in interfacing
Template D: Cut 4 pieces in Purple

2 Using an iron on a medium setting, iron on the interfacing on the WS of all fabric pieces except the four purple pieces cut from Template D, leaving a 1cm space around all sides.
3 Using a sewing machine, zigzag stitch around all pattern pieces.
Inner Bag
1 Line up the bottom of one piece A with the top of one piece B with **RS** facing.
2 Pin and stitch.
3 Iron the seams open and work the other A and B pieces the same. These sewn pieces will now be referred to as the lining bag.
4 Put the opened out lining bag pieces on top of each other with **RS** facing, making sure the seams match up. Pin the sides and bottom and stitch, leaving the space between the dotted lines open.
5 Iron the side seams open.

Straps

1 Fold one of the purple D pieces in half lengthwise. Open it up and press both sides to the fold line.
2 Fold in half once more and press.
3 Repeat for the other D pieces.
4 Pin and stitch along the long sides that are open.
5 Thread a D piece through one of the rings included on the bag straps. Fold the D piece in half, catching the ring inside it, and pin the open ends to the top of a C piece, 14cm from the side, placing so the ends are level with the top of the C piece and placed on the right side.
6 Repeat with the other side and the remaining C and D pieces.
7 Zigzag along the tops of the D pieces to secure them.

Outer Bag

1 Place the 2 C pieces on top of each other with **RS** facing. The straps will be caught inside.
2 Pin and stitch along the sides and bottom, leaving a 10cm turning gap in the bottom. This is the outer bag.
3 Keeping the piece flat, pinch the corners of the left square together at the bottom of the outer bag and make sure the edges meet.
4 Pin together and stitch. Zigzag along the edge for security.
5 Repeat for the second corner.
6 Repeat this for the bottom of the lining bag.

Assembling and joining

1 Turn the lining bag **RS** out and tuck it into the outer bag. The **RS** of the bags should be facing each other, the D-rings in between the lining and outer bag. Make sure the side seams line up.
2 Pin the tops together and stitch.
3 Pull the outer bag through the turning gap.
4 Stitch the turning gap closed and tuck the lining bag inside the outer bag.
5 Pin the top and topstitch closely along the edge.

Finishing

1 Press the bag carefully. Find the gaps in the side seam, these are to string the laces through.
2 Using tailor's chalk, draw a line along the front and back 0.5cm above the gap and 0.5cm below the gap.
3 Pin well and stitch over the chalk lines.
4 Cut the laces in half. String a lace through the front and string a piece through the back using a safety pin for assistance.
5 Sew on the button on the seam between pink and purple.
6 Give the bag one last good press and attach the handles. ♦

CLUB TROPICANA BAG PATTERN PIECES

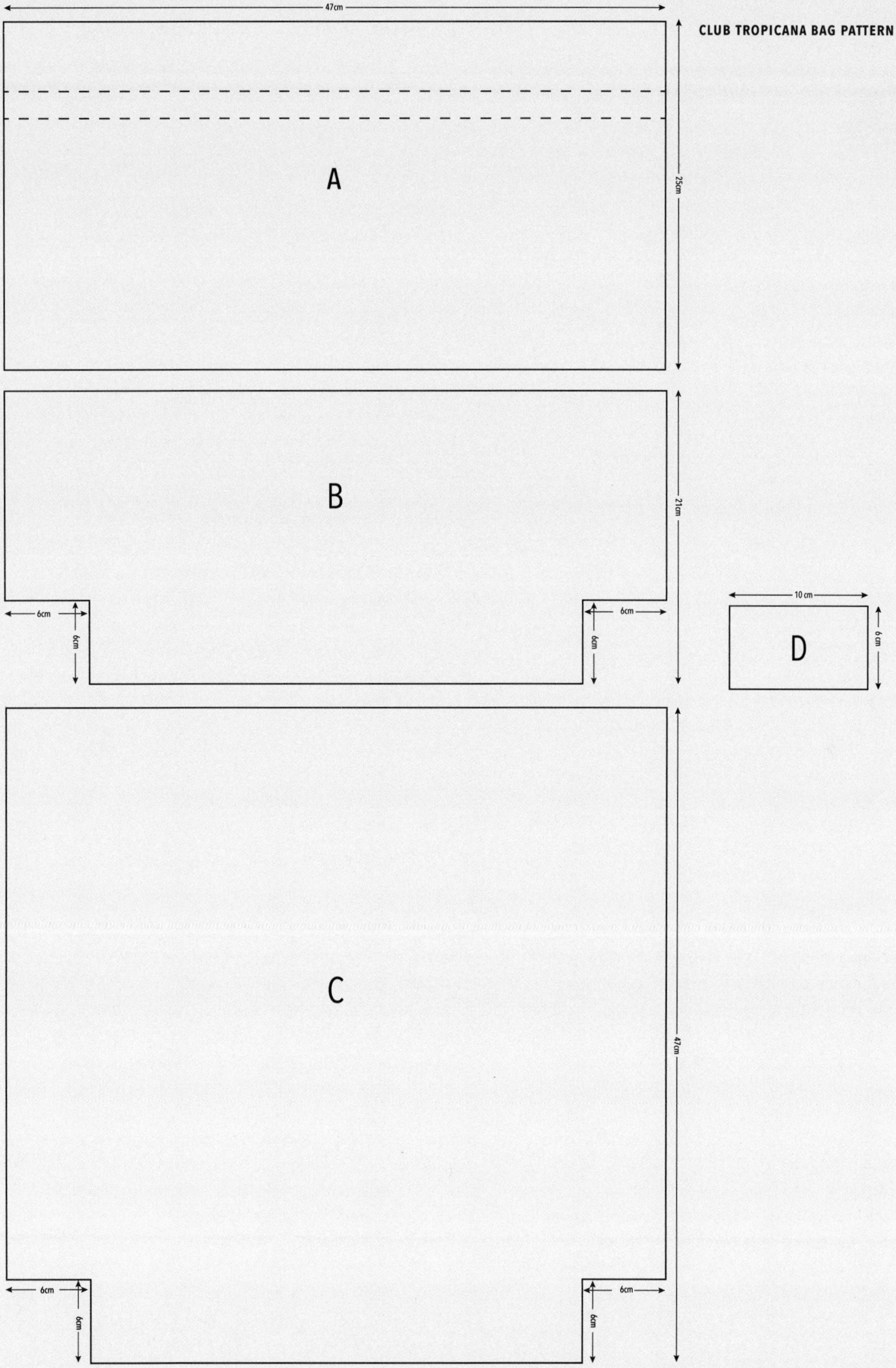

HUMMINGBIRD CARDIGAN

BY
Carmen Jorissen
craftyqueens.nl

MEASUREMENTS
S (M, L, XL)
Finished bust: 78cm (31.2in)
82: 88: 106cm (32.8: 35.2: 42.4in)
Finished length: approx. 135cm (54in)
(excluding fringe)

ABBREVIATIONS
See back cover flap

MATERIALS

Scheepjes Sunkissed (100% cotton, 50g/170m)
Yarn A: 03 Breeze x 1 ball
Yarn B: 15 Noonday Sun x 2 balls
Yarn C: 20 Beach Hut Pink x 2 balls
Yarn D: 19 Candy Floss x 2 balls
Yarn E: 07 Pistachio Ice x 2 balls
Yarn F: 18 Beach Hut Blue x 2 balls
3.5mm crochet hook

TENSION/GAUGE

A blocked single square motif measures approximately 13.5cm x 13.5cm
This pattern has a lot of positive ease

SPECIAL ABBREVIATION

Picot 6 chains, ss to base st

PATTERN NOTES

From the second square onwards, all squares are joined in the last round with the join-as-you-go method. This involves slip stitching the working square onto an already made square at certain places in the round. Change colour by finishing the last slip stitch of the round with the new colour.

INSTRUCTIONS

Square Motif

With Yarn A, make a magic ring.

Round 1 (RS) Ch4 (counts as 1 tr and 1 ch), (1tr, ch1) 11 times, ss to first tr, change to Yarn B. [12 tr, 12 ch-sps]
Round 2 Ch3 (counts as first tr), 3tr in each ch-sp to end, ss to first tr, change to Yarn C . [36 tr]
Round 3 Ss to next tr, ch3, 3tr in same space, (ch1, miss 2 tr, 4tr in next tr) 11 times, ch1, ss to first tr, change to Yarn D. [48 tr, 12 ch-sps]
Round 4 Ch4, dtr3tog over next 3 tr, yoh and pull through all loops on hook, (ch5, dtr4tog) 11 times, ch5, ss in top of first dtr cl, change to Yarn E. [12 dtr4tog, 12 ch-sps]
Round 5 (Picot) 3 times, *(ch6, ss to top of next dtr cl) 3 times, picot 3 times; rep from * twice more, (ch6, ss to top of next dtr cl) 3 times. [12 ch-6 sps, 3 picots in each corner]

Break yarn, attach Yarn F to middle picot of any corner.

Round 6 *Picot, (ch6, ss to next ch-6 sp) 3 times, ch6, ss to middle picot of next corner; rep from * twice more, (ch6, ss to next ch-6 sp) 3 times, ch6, ss to middle picot of next corner.

Break yarn and weave in all ends.

From second motif onwards, start joining the motifs as you go. See schematic for layout.

Follow these instructions for any side of a motif that should be joined:

Round 6a ch3, ss to picot on other motif, ch3, ss to base picot, *ch3, ss to ch-6 sp other motif, ch3, ss to next ch-6 sp on working motif; rep from * twice more, ch3, ss to ch-6 sp other motif, ch3, ss to next picot, ** ch3, ss to picot on other motif, ch3, ss to base picot **.

Rep these instructions if there are more sides that need to be joined. However, for two or more subsequent sides to be joined, only work the instructions between ** and ** once for each corner.

SIZE S/M/L

Attach Yarn F to outer bottom corner of left front
Round 1 1dc, (ch6, ss to next ch-sp) around edges, at a corner work 1dc in the picot then cont in patt working [ch6, ss to next ch-sp] to beg of round, ss to first dc.

SIZE S ONLY

Round 2 ch1, 1dc in top of first dc, ss in each of next 2 ch, *(ch4, ss to next ch-sp) along outer edge to top of shoulder. From this point, cont in patt until halfway around third motif. Then work (ch2, ss to corresponding ch-4 sp on other edge, ch2, ss to next ch-sp) until you reach the bottom, ss in last 2 ch, 1dc in next dc, ss in each of next 2 ch (ch4, ss to next ch-sp) from bottom hemline to next corner, ss in last 2 ch, 1dc in next dc, ss in each of next 2 ch; rep from * once more, (ch4, ss to next ch-sp) along inner edge until inner corner around neckline, ch3, ss to next ch-sp, (ch4, ss to next ch-sp) to next inner corner, ch3, ss to next ch-sp, (ch4, ss to next ch-sp) until you reach the bottom, ss in last 2 ch, 1dc in next dc, ss in each of next 2 ch, (ch4, ss to next ch-sp) to end of round.

SIZE M, L ONLY

Round 2 ch1, 1dc in top of first dc, ss in each of next 2 ch, *(ch4, ss to next ch-sp) to next corner, ss in each of last 2 ch, 1dc in next dc, ss in each of next 2 ch; rep from * around entire edge working (ch3, ss to next ch-sp) at two inner corners of neckline.

SIZE M ONLY

Round 3 Start from outer bottom corner of left front. Ch3, 1tr in next dc, 2tr over ss, (ch1, 4tr in next ch-4 sp) rep until halfway through eigth motif from the bottom, 1tr over next ss, ch1, cont around other edge, 1tr over corresponding ss on other side, 4tr in next ch-4 sp, (ss to corresponding ch-sp of other edge, 4tr in next ch-4 sp) until you reach the bottom again. Rep for the other outer edge, starting at the bottom right corner of the back.

SIZE L ONLY

Round 3 Start from outer bottom corner of left front. Ch3, 1dtr in next dc, 2dtr over ss, (ch1, 4dtr in next ch-4 sp] rep until halfway through eigth motif from the bottom, 1dtr over next ss, ch1, cont around other edge, 1dtr over corresponding ss on other side, 4dtr in next ch-4 sp, (ss to corresponding ch-sp of other edge, 4dtr in next ch-4 sp) until you reach the bottom again. Rep for the other outer edge, starting at the bottom right corner of the back.

SIZE XL ONLY

Round 1 Around both armholes and along bottom hemline: Attach yarn with 1dc in any picot, (ch6, ss to next ch-sp) rep until you reach either the beg of the round again (for armholes) or the other end of the bottom hem.

Round 2 For both armholes: ss to any ch-6 sp, (ch4, ss to next ch-sp) around.

For bottom hem: Ch1, 1dc on top of first dc, ss in each of next 2 ch, (ch4, ss to next ch-sp) rep to next corner, ss in each of last 2 ch, 1dc in dc.

ALL SIZES

Attach Yarn A to inner corner of right front, ch2, 1htr in next dc, 1htr in each of next 2 ss, (ch1, 4htr in next ch-sp) rep all around inner edge until you reach the bottom again, 1htr in each of last 2 ss, 2htr in next dc.

TO FINISH

Weave in all ends.

To add fringes to the bottom hem, cut pieces of approx. 16cm of Yarn F. If there is not enough left of Yarn F, you could also partly use Yarn A. The cardigan shown here has 29 fringes of 5 pieces each, distributed evenly along the bottom hem. To attach the fringe, fold the cut pieces in half, place a crochet hook through the gap you want to attach it to, pull the loop through the gap and put the ends through the loop. Pull tight. Rep for the rest of the fringes, trim edges if required. ♦

HUMMINGBIRD CARDIGAN LAYOUT

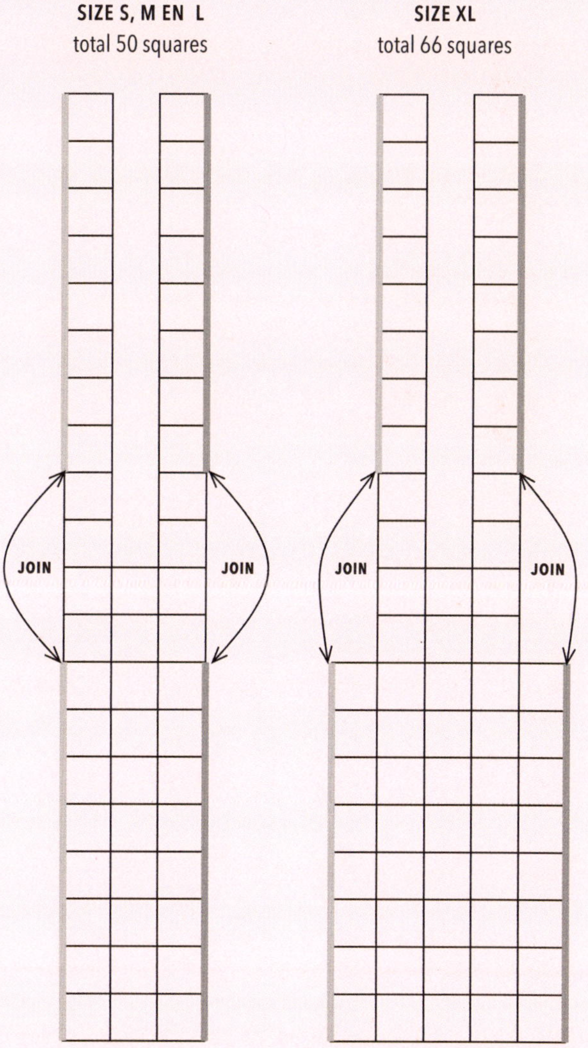

MANHATTAN CLUTCH

BY
Sarah Knight
craftsfromthecwtch.co.uk

MEASUREMENTS
26 x 26cm
(10.4in x 10.4in)
Open 38cm (15in)

ABBREVIATIONS
See back cover flap

MATERIALS

Scheepjes Secret Garden (20% silk, 20% cotton, 60% polyester, 50g/93m)
Yarn A: 705 Rambling Blooms x 1 ball
Yarn B: 702 Herb Garden x 1 ball
3.5mm knitting needles
Tapestry needle
Bag clasp - Opry art. 99643-Z
27 x 75cm (10 x 29½in) fabric art. 96058 Tissu de Marie-Stof 100% polyester-cotton in colour 7
27 x 75cm (10 x 29½in) lightweight quilter's wadding
1 x Gütterman thread in col 258
Sewing machine, pins and basic sewing supplies

GAUGE/TENSION

22 sts and 25 rows to 10 x 10cm in stocking stitch, using 3.5mm needles.

SPECIAL ABBREVIATION

sl1wyif slip the stated number of stitches from the left to right needle, as if to purl. When slipping stitches, the yarn should always be held to wrong side of work, so on **WS** rows slip the stitch(es) with the yarn in front.

PATTERN NOTES

The colour work front and back are worked from the top down using slipped stitches and just one yarn at a time. The two knitted pieces are sewn together to add structure. A fabric lining (with interfacing) is added before sewing the body to the silver clutch clasp.
The closure flap is folded onto the front of the bag, before the final seams are sewn.

INSTRUCTIONS

Front/Back

Make two, starting new yarn balls at the beginning of each piece.
With Yarn A, cast on 43 sts.
Begin with a k row, work in st st for 2.5cm (1in), then start the colour work pattern from written or charted instructions below.

Row 1 (RS) With A, knit.
Row 2 With A, purl.
Row 3 Change to Yarn B, k2, (sl3, k3) to last 5 sts, sl3, k2.
Row 4 With B, p3, (sl1 wyif, p5) to last 4 sts, sl1, p3.
Row 5 With B, knit.
Row 6 With B, purl.
Row 7 Change to Yarn A, k5, (sl3, k3) to last 2 sts, k2.
Row 8 With A, p6, (sl1 wyif, p5) to last st, p1.
Rep Rows 1 to 8 four times, then increase as follows:

Inc row (RS) With A, cast on 6 sts using cable cast on, k to end. [49 sts]
Next row With A, cast on 6 sts using cable cast on, p to end. [55 sts]
Rep rows 1 to 8 nine times.
Next row (RS) With A, knit.
Next row With A, purl.
Next row Change to Yarn B, k2, (sl3, k3) to last 5 sts, sl3, k2.
Next row With B, p3, (sl1 wyif, p5) to last 4 sts, sl1, p3.
Next row With B, knit.
Next row With B, purl.
Rep last two rows five times.
Cast off and sew in ends.

Joining

Using mattress stitch and leftover yarn, sew the two pieces together along the long edges and bottom, leaving the shorter top edges open along three sides (this is used to attach to the clasp).

Lining

The finished lining should fit perfectly into the metal handle and into the knitted outer. Check against these as you go along.

Step 1 With **RS** of fabric showing, sew the wadding to the back on the fabric along all four sides, leaving a 1cm (0.5in) seam allowance.
Step 2 With **RS's** of fabric together, insert lining into the knitted outer and mark exactly the position of the opening, using pins.
Step 3 Remove lining from the knitted outer, and sew the lining together up to the pinned marker on both sides.

MANHATTAN CLUTCH COLOURS AND STITCH PATTERN

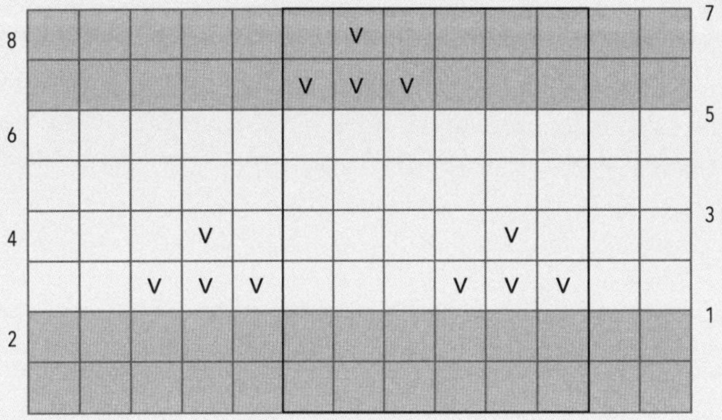

Rambling Blooms
Herb Garden
RS: knit / WS: purl
V RS: slip / WS: slip purlwise with yarn in front
Pattern reapeat

Step 4 Fold the top edge along the stitches, and top stitch very close to the edge.
Step 5 Fold along the stitches on the side openings and top stitch. Aside from the corners, the lining should now be a perfect fit for the handle.
Step 6 Mark 1cm (0.5in) to either side of the corner then draw a line between the marks. Sew alongside the line, leaving a small seam allowance, to secure the other seams and then cut off the excess fabric along the line.
Step 7 Place the lining into the knitted outer and pin them together along the sides. Note that the fabric will buckle slightly until it is attached to the clasp.
Step 8 Hand-stitch along the sides to secure the lining and outer together. Then do the same along each of the top edges and corners, taking care to position the knitted outer to match the size of the lining.

Attaching bag to clasp

Carefully insert the top edges into the metal clasp and secure with sewing thread and needle. You may find it easier to secure the central holes on each side of the clasp first, and to work outwards.

Decide which will be the front of the bag, then fold the clasp section over to rest on the front. Finally, using sewing thread and needle, stitch the openings beneath the clasp hinge neatly closed and secure the front flap in place. ♦

PIÑA COLADA SHAWL

BY
Nerissa Muijs
missneriss.com

MEASUREMENTS
Width: 175cm (69in)
Depth: 80cm (31.5in)

ABBREVIATIONS
See back cover flap

MATERIALS

Scheepjes Secret Garden (20% silk, 20% cotton, 60% polyester, 50g/93m)
Yarn A: 707 Summer House x 6 balls
Yarn B: 706 Blossom x 5 balls
5mm crochet hook

TENSION/GAUGE

15 sts and 9 rows in treble crochet to 10 x 10cm (4 x 4in) using 5mm hook or size required to obtain tension.

SPECIAL ABBREVIATIONS

dcInc 2 double crochet in one stitch (increase)
htrInc 2 half treble crochet in one stitch (increase)
trInc 2 treble crochet in one stitch (increase)

PATTERN NOTES

This pattern is worked back and forth in rows in the shape of a semi-circle. Short rows create the blended colours. The first full set of repeats will always be in trebles, the second will be half trebles, and the rest of the repeats will be where the shaping and short rows are. When slip stitching, make sure it is done loosely to avoid pulling. The ch2 at the start of each row beginning with a treble does not count as a stitch. Upon completing each row, turn and work back the other way.

When finishing a slip stitch row, make the very last stitch from back to the front of the loops instead of front to back, this will make the turn invisible. At the beginning of a slip stitch row, pull the loop on the hook to be a little looser than usual, and miss the first stitch. On the last row of the colour section, make your stitch through to the stitch in the row below where that missed stitch sits. Consider adding a half treble in that stitch when finishing the row, it helps with blending the short rows. When changing colours, always start at the end where the short rows finish, attaching the yarn to the first stitch of the last row of the same colour.

If the increases begin to appear directly above one another, which can happen as exact counting isn't crucial, offset the increases by 10 stitches in either direction. This will prevent corners forming – notice that some of the counts are a bit unusual because of this.

INSTRUCTIONS

Yarn A

Row 1 Ch4, ss in fourth ch to make a ring, ch2, 3tr, 4htr, 3tr in ring. [10 sts]
Row 2 TrInc in first st, 1tr, (htrInc in next st, 1htr in next st) 3 times, trInc, 1tr, turn (at end of this row and throughout). [15 sts]
Row 3 TrInc, 2tr, (htrInc, 2htr) 3 times, trInc, 2tr. [20 sts]
Row 4 TrInc, 3tr, (htrInc, 3htr) 3 times, trInc, 3tr. [25 sts]
Row 5 TrInc, 4tr, (htrInc, 4htr) 3 times, trInc, 4tr. [30 sts]
Row 6 TrInc, 5tr, (htrInc, 5htr) 3 times, trInc, 5tr. [35 sts]
Fasten off.

Yarn B

Row 1 Ch2, trInc, 6tr, (htrInc, 6htr) 3 times, dcInc, 6dc. [40 sts]
Row 2 Miss 1, 5ss, 7dc, (htrInc, 7htr) twice, trInc, 7tr, trInc, 2tr.
Row 3 TrInc, 8tr, (htrInc, 8htr) twice, htrInc, 4htr, 4dc, dcInc, 3dc, ss.
Row 4 Miss 1, 5ss, 9dc, htrInc, 9htr, htrInc, 5tr, trInc, 9tr.
Row 5 TrInc, 10tr, (htrInc, 10htr) twice, dcInc, 3dc, ss.
Row 6 Miss 1, 5ss, 5dc, htrInc, 11htr, trInc, 11tr, trInc, 6tr.
Row 7 TrInc, 12tr, htrInc, 6htr, 6dc, dcInc, 12dc, dcInc, 15dc, ss.
Fasten off.

Yarn A

Row 1 TrInc, 12tr, (htrInc, 12htr) twice, dcInc, 12dc, dcInc, 5dc, ss.
Row 2 Miss 1, 5ss, 13dc, (htrInc, 13htr) twice, trInc, 10tr, trInc, 5tr.
Row 3 TrInc, 14tr, (htrInc, 14htr) twice, dcInc, 10dc, ss.
Row 4 Miss 1, 5ss, 15dc, htrInc, 15htr, trInc, 15tr, trInc, 7tr.
Row 5 TrInc, 16tr, htrInc, 16htr, htrInc, 8htr, 8dc, dcInc, ss.
Row 6 Miss 1, 5ss, 17dc, 2htr, 17htr, trInc, 15tr.
Row 7 TrInc, 18tr, htrInc, 18htr, (dcInc, 18dc) twice, ss.
Fasten off.

Yarn B

Row 1 TrInc, 19tr, (trInc, 19htr) twice, dcInc, 19dc, ss.
Row2 Miss 1, 5ss, 20dc, (htrInc, 20htr) twice, trInc, 16tr.
Row 3 TrInc, 21tr, htrInc, 21htr, htrInc, 11htr, 10dc, dcInc, 10dc, ss.
Row 4 Miss 1, 5ss, 22dc, htrInc, 22htr, trInc, 22tr, trInc, 7tr.
Row 5 TrInc, 23tr, htrInc, 23htr, htrInc, 12htr, 11dc, ss.
Row 6 Miss 1, 5ss, 24dc, htrInc, 12htr, trInc, 24tr, trInc, 6tr.
Row 7 TrInc, 25tr, htrInc, 25htr, dcInc, 26dc, dcInc, 14dc, ss.
Fasten off.

Yarn A

Row 1 TrInc, 27tr, htrInc, 27htr, htrInc, 20htr, 7dc, dcInc, 20dc, ss.
Row 2 Miss 1, 5ss, 28dc, htrInc, 28htr, htrInc, 20htr, 8tr, trInc, 17tr.
Row 3 TrInc, 29tr, htrInc, 29htr, htrInc, 10htr, 19dc, dcInc, 10dc, ss.
Row 4 Miss 1, 5ss, 30dc, htrInc, 30htr, trInc, 30tr, trInc, 7tr.
Row 5 TrInc, 31tr, htrInc, 31htr, dcInc, 31dc, dcInc, ss.
Row 6 Miss 1, 5ss, 32dc, htrInc, 32htr, trInc, 30tr.
Row 7 TrInc, 33tr, htrInc, 33htr, dcInc, 33dc, dcInc, 19dc, ss.
Fasten off.

Yarn B

Row 1 TrInc, 34tr, htrInc, 34htr, htrInc, 20htr, 14dc, dcInc, 18dc, ss.
Row 2 Miss 1, 5ss, 35dc, htrInc, 35htr, htrInc, 20htr, 15tr, trInc, 15tr.
Row 3 TrInc, 36tr, htrInc, 36htr, htrInc, 10htr, 26dc, dcInc, 8dc, ss.
Row 4 Miss 1, 5ss, 37dc, htrInc, 37htr, trInc, 37tr, trInc, 5tr.
Row 5 TrInc, 38tr, htrInc, 38htr, dcInc, 37dc, ss.
Row 6 Miss 1, 5ss, 39dc, htrInc, 39htr, trInc, 34tr.
Row 7 TrInc, 40tr, htrInc, 40htr, dcInc, 40dc, dcInc, 16dc, ss.
Fasten off.

Yarn A

Row 1 TrInc, 41tr, htrInc, 41htr, htrInc, 20htr, 21dc, dcInc, 19dc, ss.
Row 2 Miss 1, 5ss, 42dc, htrInc, 42htr, trInc, 42tr, trInc, 16tr.
Row 3 TrInc, 43tr, htrInc, 43htr, htrInc, 10htr, 23dc, dcInc, 18dc, ss.
Row 4 Miss 1, 5ss, 44dc, htrInc, 44htr, trInc, 44tr, trInc, 2tr.
Row 5 TrInc, 45tr, htrInc, 45htr, dcInc, 43dc, ss.
Row 6 Miss 1, 5ss, 46dc, htrInc, 46htr, trInc, 40tr.
Row 7 TrInc, 47tr, htrInc, 47htr, dcInc, 47dc, dcInc, 16dc, ss.
Fasten off.

Yarn B

Row 1 TrInc, 48tr, htrInc, 48htr, htrInc, 20htr, 28dc, dcInc, 15dc, ss.
Row 2 Miss 1, 5ss, 49dc, htrInc, 49htr, trInc, 49tr, trInc, 14tr.
Row 3 TrInc, 50tr, htrInc, 50htr, htrInc, 10htr, 40dc, dcInc, 5dc, ss.
Row 4 Miss 1, 5ss, 55dc, htrInc, 51htr, trInc, 50tr.
Row 5 TrInc, 52tr, htrInc, 52htr, dcInc, 47dc, ss.
Row 6 Miss 1, 5ss, 53dc, htrInc, 53htr, trInc, 45tr.
Row 7 TrInc, 54tr, htrInc, 44htr, 10dc, dcInc, 38dc, ss.
Row 8 Miss 1, 5ss, 55dc, htrInc, 55htr, trInc, 35tr.
Row 9 TrInc, 56tr, htrInc, 30htr, 26dc, dcInc, 56dc, dcInc, 11dc, ss.
Fasten off.

Yarn A

Row 1 TrInc, 57tr, htrInc, 57htr, htrInc, 20htr, 37dc, dcInc, 11dc, ss.
Row 2 Miss 1, 5ss, 58dc, htrInc, 58htr, trInc, 58tr, trInc, 8tr.
Row 3 TrInc, 59tr, htrInc, 59htr, htrInc, 10htr, 49dc, ss.
Row 4 Miss 1, 5ss, 60dc, htrInc, 6htr, trInc, 59tr.
Row 5 TrInc, 61tr, htrInc, 61htr, dcInc, 51dc, ss.
Row 6 Miss 1, 5ss, 62dc, htrInc, 62htr, trInc, 48tr.
Row 7 TrInc, 63tr, htrInc, 53htr, 10dc, dcInc, 41dc, ss.
Row 8 Miss 1, 5ss, 64dc, htrInc, 64htr, trInc, 38tr.
Row 9 TrInc, 65tr, htrInc, 30htr, 35dc, dcInc, 65dc, dcInc, 7dc, ss.
Fasten off.

Yarn B

Row 1 TrInc, 66tr, htrInc, 66htr, htrInc, 20htr, 46dc, dcInc, 10dc, ss.
Row 2 Miss 1, 5ss, 60dc, htrInc, 67htr, trInc, 67tr, trInc, 14tr.
Row 3 TrInc, 68tr, htrInc, 68htr, htrInc, 10htr, 58dc, dcInc, 67dc, ss.
Row 4 Miss 1, 5ss, 50dc, htrInc, 69htr, trInc, 69tr, trInc, 15tr.
Row 5 TrInc, 70tr, htrInc, 70htr, dcInc, 60dc, ss.
Row 6 Miss 1, 5ss, 71dc, htrInc, 71htr, trInc, 57tr.
Row 7 TrInc, 72tr, htrInc, 61htr, 10dc, dcInc, 50dc, ss.
Row 8 Miss 1, 5ss, 73dc, htrInc, 73htr, trInc, 47tr.
Row 9 TrInc, 74tr, htrInc, 30htr, 45dc, dcInc, 74dc, dcInc, 7dc, ss.
Fasten off.

Yarn A

Row 1 TrInc, 75tr, htrInc, 75htr, htrInc, 20htr, 55dc, dcInc, 75dc, dcInc, 3dc, ss.
Row 2 Miss 1, 5ss, 60dc, htrInc, 76htr, trInc, 76tr, trInc, 17tr.
Row 3 TrInc, 77tr, htrInc, 77htr, htrInc, 10htr, 72dc, ss.
Row 4 Miss 1, 5ss, 78dc, htrInc, 78htr, htrInc, 68tr.
Row 5 TrInc, 79tr, htrInc, 79htr, dcInc, 61dc, ss.
Row 6 Miss 1, 5ss, 80dc, htrInc, 80htr, trInc, 58tr.
Row 7 TrInc, 81tr, htrInc, 81htr, htrInc, 17htr, 10dc, dcInc, 51dc, ss.
Row 8 Miss 1, 5ss, 82dc, htrInc, 60htr, trInc, 70tr.
Row 9 TrInc, 83tr, htrInc, 83htr, dcInc, 83dc, dcInc, 1dc, ss.
Fasten off.

Yarn B

Row 1 TrInc, 84tr, htrInc, 84htr, htrInc, 20htr, 64dc, dcInc, 84dc, dcInc, 1dc, ss.
Row 2 Miss 1, 5ss, 60dc, htrInc, 85htr, trInc, 85tr, trInc, 24tr.
Row 3 TrInc, 86tr, htrInc, 86htr, htrInc, 10htr, 77dc, ss.
Row 4 Miss 1, 5ss, 87dc, htrInc, 87htr, trInc, 73tr.
Row 5 TrInc, 88tr, htrInc, 88htr, dcInc, 66dc, ss.
Row 6 Miss 1, 5ss, 89dc, htrInc, 89htr, trInc, 63tr.
Row 7 TrInc, 90tr, htrInc, 80htr, 10dc, dcInc, 56dc.
Row 8 Miss 1, 5ss, 91dc, htrInc, 80htr, trInc, 64tr.
Row 9 TrInc, 92tr, htrInc, 92htr, dcInc, 88dc, ss.
Fasten off.

Yarn B

Row 1 TrInc, 93tr, htrInc, 93htr, htrInc, 20htr, 73dc, dcInc, 92dc, ss.
Row 2 Miss 1, 5ss, 60dc, htrInc, 94htr, trInc, 94tr, trInc, 29tr.
Row 3 TrInc, 95tr, htrInc, 95htr, htrInc, 10htr, 81dc, ss.
Row 4 Miss 1, 5ss, 96dc, htrInc, 96htr, trInc, 79tr.
Row 5 TrInc, 97tr, htrInc, 87htr, 10dc, dcInc, 71dc, ss.
Row 6 Miss 1, 5ss, 98dc, htrInc, 98htr, trInc, 68tr.
Row 7 TrInc, 99tr, htrInc, 79htr, 20dc, dcInc, 61dc.
Row 8 Miss 1, 5ss, 100dc, htrInc, 70htr, trInc, 82tr.
Row 9 TrInc, 101tr, htrInc, 101htr, dcInc, 90dc, ss.
Fasten off.

PICOT EDGING

With Yarn A, start at the end of very first section; work across Yarn A side to corner, then around the crescent until reaching Yarn B. Change to Yarn B and continue to the corner, then back to meet the start of the edging. Use the following stitch repeat: (ss, ch3, ss) in the same stitch, dc in the next.

TO FINISH

Soak in Eucalan and block the shawl quite aggressively horizontally, pulling the flat edge as far as possible. While wet on the board, smooth the colours into nice round lines to eliminate any corners. ♦

MOJITO ESPADRILLES

BY
Nerissa Muijs
missneriss.com

SIZE
36/37 (38/39)
UK Size 3-4 (5-6)

ABBREVIATIONS
See back cover flap

MATERIALS

Scheepjes Maxi Sugar Rush 392 Lime Juice (100% mercerized cotton, 50g/280m) x 1 ball
Scheepjes Maxi Bonbon 398 Colonial Rose (100% mercerized cotton, 25g/140m) x 1 ball
Prym Espadrille soles (art. 975 200 – 975 209) in size 36/37 (38/39)
3mm crochet hook
Needle to attach fabric to soles
4m band (art. 2138, colour 638 yellow)

TENSION/GAUGE

Double crochet
24 sts and 24 rows to 10 x 10cm over double crochet using 3 strands of yarn and 3mm hook or size required to obtain tension.

SPECIAL ABBREVIATIONS

dc2tog 2 double crochet stitches together to decrease 1 stitch
dc3tog 3 double crochet stitches together to decrease 2 stitches

PATTERN NOTES

This pattern is worked back and forth in rows using the yarn triple stranded. At the end of each row, chain 1 and turn your work. When attaching the front part of the shoe fabric to the sole, fold it under a little to help create the height and rounded look of the shoe. Use blanket stitch to attach fabric to the sole. Please note that the pattern may need some adjusting to suit individual foot shape and size. For larger or wider sizes, simply do not fold the side seams under. The stitch will have some give. For a firmer fit, make the size smaller.

INSTRUCTIONS

Toe

With 3 strands of **Sugar Rush** and 3mm hook, work ch29 (31).

Foundation row Dc in second st from hook and next 27 (29) ch. [28 (30) dc]
Row 1 Dc to end.
Row 2 2dc in first dc, dc to last st, 2dc in last st. [30 (32) dc]
Rows 3-4 Dc to end.
Row 5 2dc in first dc, dc to last st, 2dc in last st. [32 (34) dc]
Rows 6-7 Dc to end.
Row 8 2dc in first dc, dc to last st, 2dc in last st. [34 (36) dc]
Rows 9-10 Dc to end.

SIZE 38/39 ONLY

Row 11 2dc in first dc, dc in the next 34 sts, 2dc in last st. [38 dc]
Rows 12-13 Dc to end.

BOTH SIZES

Change to 3 strands of **Bonbon**
Row 11 (14) 2dc in first dc, dc to last st, 2dc in last st. [36 (40) dc]
Row 12 (15) 5htr, 26 (30)dc, 5htr.
Row 13 (16) Dc to end.
Row 14 (17) 3htr, 30 (34)dc, 3htr.
Row 15 (18) Dc to end.
Row 16 (19) 10htr, 16 (20)dc, 10htr.
Row 17 (20) Dc to end.

Heel

With 3 strands of **Sugar Rush** and 3mm hook, work ch35 (37).

Foundation row Dc in second st from hook and next 33 (35) ch. [34 (36) dc]

Rows 1-3 Dc to end.
Row 4 16 (17)dc, dc2tog, 16 (17)dc. [33 (35) dc]
Row 5 1dc, 2dc in next st, dc to last 2 sts, 2dc in next st, 1dc. [35 (37) dc]
Rows 6-8 Dc to end.
Row 9 1dc, 2dc in next st, dc to last 2 sts, 2dc in next st, 1dc. [37 (39) dc]
Rows 10-11 Dc to end.

Change to 3 strands of **Bonbon**

Row 12 1dc, 2dc in next st, 15 (16)dc, dc3tog, 15 (16)dc, 2dc in next st, 1dc. [37 (39) dc]
Rows 13-14 Dc to end.
Row 15 Dc2tog, dc to last 2 sts, dc2tog. [35 (37) dc]
Row 16 Dc2tog, 14 (15)dc, dc3tog, 14 (15)dc, 2dctog. [31 (33) dc]
Row 17 (WS) Dc2tog, dc to last 2 sts, dc2tog. [29 (31) dc]
Fasten off.

EMBELLISHMENT

Toe

Using one strand of **Bonbon**, work surface ss along **RS** in **Sugar Rush** section, 1 row down from colour change from one side to the other. Rep twice more, spacing them evenly, two rows apart.

Heel

Using one strand of **Bonbon**, surface ss along **RS** in **Sugar Rush** section, 1 row down from colour change from one side to the other. Weave in ends.

ASSEMBLY

Heel

Using blanket stitch and 3 strands of yarn, start sewing heel (**Sugar Rush** section) 6.5 (7)cm from back of heel. Work around back of the heel, keeping heel fabric tight and ensure that it ends evenly at 6.5 (7)cm on the other side.
Note: make sure the embellishment stripes are facing outwards.

Toe

Using blanket stitch and 3 strands of **Bonbon**, fold the edge slightly under (about 1 stitch) and work along the side, 11 (13)cm from point of toe on inside edge and 13 (14)cm on outside edge.). Change thread colour when reaching **Sugar Rush** section. Continue to end of **Sugar Rush** edge, ss across toe fabric and down the other side – folding the edge slightly under to improve shape and give firm fit. Change to **Bonbon** when the colour changes, stitch to end, ss across fabric, join and fasten off.

Band

Cut band into four equal lengths of at least 1m. Sew each end (single stranded) to corners of heel fabric on a 45 degree angle. Tie around ankles or up the leg – ballerina style.

Alternative strap: from inside corner of heel fabric, using 3 strands of yarn work ch25, 1dc in fifth ch from hook and in each ch to end. Attach a button to outside corner adjusting size of loop to fit button.
♦

TEQUILA SUNRISE TOWELS

BY
Maria McPherson
justahappyhooker.blogspot.co.uk

MEASUREMENTS
Towel width 70cm (28in)
Border 6cm (2.4in)

ABBREVIATIONS
See back cover flap

MATERIALS

Scheepjes Maxi Bonbon (100% mercerized cotton, 25g/140m)

Colour Option 1
1 ball each of:
Yarn A: 101 Candle Light
Yarn B: 255 Nude
Yarn C: 414 Salmon
Yarn D: 264 Light Coral
Yarn E: 410 Rich Coral
Yarn F: 256 Cornelia Rose
Yarn G: 413 Cherry

Colour Option 2
1 ball each of:
Yarn A: 101 Candle Light
Yarn B: 392 Lime Juice
Yarn C: 404 English Tea
Yarn D: 403 Lemonade
Yarn E: 208 Yellow Gold
Yarn F: 411 Sweet Orange
Yarn G: 386 Peach

Both Options
Bath Towel
2.5mm crochet hook
Tapestry needle
Ruler
Fading marker pen
Scissors

SPECIAL ABBREVIATION

P (special picot) (1dc, 1ch, 1dc) in same stitch

INSTRUCTIONS

With a fading marker pen and ruler, make a line of dots, in multiples of 6 + 1, at 1cm intervals and approximately 0.5cm in from towel edge.
Using Yarn A and tapestry needle, work a row of blanket stitch along the towel edge.

Row 1 (RS) Using 2.5mm hook and Yarn A, make a sl knot on hook and work 1dc under first vertical of blanket stitch to join in yarn, *2dc in horizontal of blanket stitch, dc under both vertical and horizontal of blanket stitch; rep from * to end, ch1, turn.
Row 2 (WS) 1dc in first st, (ch3, miss 2 sts, 1dc) to end, ch2, turn.
Row 3 (2dc in ch-3 sp, ch2) to end, 1dc in last st.
Fasten off.
Row 4 Using Yarn B, ch3, (1dc in ch-sp, ch3) to last st, 1dc in last st.
Fasten off.
Row 5 Using Yarn C, ch1, 1dc in first st, (2dc in ch-sp, 1dc) to end.
Fasten off.
Row 6 Using Yarn D, ch3 (counts as first st), *1tr, miss next 3 sts (2tr, ch1, 2tr) in next st; rep from * to last st, 2tr in last st.
Fasten off.
Row 7 Using Yarn E, ch3 (counts as first st), 1tr in first st, ((2tr, ch1, 2tr) in ch-sp) to last st, 2tr in last st. Fasten off.
Row 8 Using Yarn F, as Row 7.
Row 9 Using Yarn G, ch3, 3tr in first st, *miss 3 sts, 1dc in next ch-sp, miss 3 sts, 7tr in next ch-sp; rep from, * to last 4 sts, miss 3 sts, 4tr in last st, ch1, turn.
Row 10 P in first st, *ch3, miss 3 sts, 1dc in next dc, ch3, miss 3 sts, P in fourth of 7 tr; rep from * to last st, P in last st.
Fasten off.

TO FINISH

Rep for other end of towel.
Weave in ends and block to finish. ♦

NOTES

NOTES

NOTES

SCRAPBOOK

stick your swatches, cuttings, yarn bands, inspirational pictures, etc. here